GEONOMICS INSTITUTE FOR INTERNATIONAL ECONOMIC
ADVANCEMENT SERIES
Michael P. Claudon, Series Editor

Debt Disaster? Banks, Governments, and Multilaterals Confront the Crisis
edited by John F. Weeks

*The Canada-U.S. Free Trade Agreement: Implications, Opportunities,
and Challenges*
edited by Daniel E. Nolle

Perestroika and East-West Economic Relations: Prospects for the 1990's
edited by Michael Kraus and Ronald D. Liebowitz

Reforming the Ruble: Monetary Aspects of Perestroika
edited by Josef C. Brada and Michael P. Claudon

*The Emerging Russian Bear: Integrating the Soviet Union into the
World Economy*
edited by Josef C. Brada and Michael P. Claudon

The Emerging Russian Bear

Integrating the Soviet Union into the World Economy

Edited by Josef C. Brada
and Michael P. Claudon

NEW YORK UNIVERSITY PRESS
New York and London

Library of Congress Cataloging-in-Publication Data

The Emerging Russian Bear : integrating the Soviet Union into the
world economy / edited by Josef C. Brada and Michael P. Claudon.
        p.   cm. — (Geonomics Institute for International Economic
Advancement series)
     Includes index.
     ISBN 0-8147-1458-7
     1. Soviet Union—Commercial policy—Congresses.   2. Soviet Union—
Foreign economic relations—Congresses.   3. Commercial law—Soviet
Union—Congresses.   4. Soviet Union—Economic policy—1986—Congresses.
I. Brada, Josef C., 1942-   . II. Claudon, Michael P.   III. Series.
HF1557.E54 1991
337.41—dc20   91-10320
                                                                      CIP

New York University Press books are printed on acid-free paper,
and their binding materials are chosen for strength and durability.

Contents

Acknowledgments

Many have contributed to the success of this East-West venture. In the first place, this volume has benefited from the generosity of the conference sponsors: Dun & Bradstreet Corporation; Heytesbury Inc.; Institute for the Study of the USA and Canada (Moscow); International Bank Credit Analysts; Jones International, Inc.; Henry Kaufman & Company, Inc.; MMS International, Inc.; New York Stock Exchange, Inc.; Schooner Capital Corporation; Scott European Corporation; and Sharpoint. The conference also benefited from the participation of a large and diverse group of specialists on East-West relations.

The staff of the Geonomics Institute, including Nancy Ward, Elizabeth Leeds, and George Bellerose, ably assisted in organizing and executing many aspects of the conference program. Colleen Duncan provided editorial assistance and shepherded the preparations of the volume for publication from the May 1990 conference through several stages of revisions, to this updated final version. Their contributions are invaluable.

ix

Foreword

In 1985, following a decade of stagnating economic performance, Mikhail S. Gorbachev rose from relative obscurity to become General Secretary of the Communist Party, shocking his own people and the world by admitting what had been obvious to many western observers for some time: Socialism, so cherished by Lenin for its guarantee of equity, had proved unequal to the task of directing a modern, industrial economy. The certainty provided by centralized planning, artificial prices, and the ultimate welfare state had proved its mettle at transforming a largely peasant society into the second largest industrialized economy in the world.

Equally certain, however, was the fact that in a modern, complex, industrialized economy, socialism could not deliver private-sector goods and services in sufficient quantities, respond to the ebb and flow of peoples' wants, or generate sufficient economic growth to perpetuate, let alone improve, living standards.

Now, six years later, we are still asking the same litany of questions: Can President Gorbachev transform a moribund planned economy dominated by inefficient state monopolies into a competitive, market-oriented one dominated by private firms? Can an autarkic Soviet Union, after years of Cold War economic isolation, be integrated into the world economy? Can the Soviet Union quickly develop the financial and legal infrastructure needed in a market-oriented economy? Indeed, is the hibernating Russian Bear reawakening?

As of this writing, answers to these questions continue to bedevil Gorbachev. Moreover, increasingly strident calls for independence among the federated republics are distracting the union government from its central task: putting food and consumer goods in stores at prices within the reach of average Soviet workers. How to produce results quickly is no longer only a scholar's question. Gorbachev's inability to break the logjam is beginning to raise the specter of a central government without a structure within which to govern.

When I met with Boris Yeltsin's vice president, Ruslan Khasbulatov, in September 1990, I was struck by President Gorbachev's paradoxical situation. His formal powers and international reputation have never been greater, but his ability to govern is under siege from within his own country. However incorrectly, republic leaders contend that he and the Soviet Union have become irrelevant. He is being held accountable from all quarters for centuries-old attitudes and the failures of three generations, as well as for his inability to correct them overnight.

It is undeniable that five years into perestroika the Soviet economy is in desperate shape. Growing despair and anxiety are widespread—in conversations, in queues, in the weariness of people in the streets. When in Moscow, I repeatedly hear the same pessimistic refrain: "Now we have higher wages and, in some cases, better working conditions and more personal freedom. But we are not living as well. What good is money when the state stores are empty, and the black marketeers, cooperatives, and farmers' markets charge such high prices that we can actually buy less now than we could before 1985?"

Retail shelves are empty, while city apartments and homes in the Moscow *oblast* overflow with stores of nonperishable food, consumer goods, jewelry, and antiques. People are hoarding commodities to hedge against expected inflation. In agricultural areas, farmers, rather than obey state orders, are storing their harvests for sale at expected higher winter prices. They will eat their own produce or feed it to their animals before participating in a discredited centralized system. At least in this one sense the situation is not quite as desperate as it seems when one confronts the empty state stores on Gorky Street. But the fact that central planning has largely collapsed is inescapable.

Real economic power is devolving away from the central ministries and the bureaucracy to local authorities. State enterprises, private cooperatives, and new joint-stock companies are producing for and bartering directly with each other, or selling openly in the dollar markets springing up everywhere, rather than delivering goods ordered by the central planners. President Gorbachev's authority is being seriously undermined, and his recent decree notwithstanding, enterprises are not fulfilling state orders.

It is against this backdrop that the Geonomics Institute presents the following proceedings of its May 1990 seminar, "Financial Markets, Joint Ventures, and Business Opportunities in the Soviet Union." The forty participants grappled with a wide range of issues, all tied together by a common thread: How and when will this potential powerhouse be integrated into the world economy?

This volume contributes exceptionally well to Geonomics' mission to bring together business leaders, government policymakers, and academicians. Geonomics seeks to devise workable and creative solutions to the fundamental economic and development problems faced by emerging democracies that build on western business and economic success. Geonomics is privately funded, nonpartisan, and not for profit. We welcome ideas and opinions for better achieving our goals.

Michael P. Claudon
President and Managing Director
Geonomics Institute

Introduction

President Gorbachev's apparent lack of tangible results to date must be judged against the reality that no country has attempted economic and political reforms on so massive a scale as has the Soviet Union during the past five years. It is hardly surprising in such a large and culturally diverse country that the Soviets face enormous obstacles: a recalcitrant bureaucracy, inefficient and uncompetitive state monopolies, a lack of consumer goods, repressed inflation, an inadequate infrastructure, poor worker morale, and a general lack of incentives throughout the economy.

The Soviet Union has begun to reach out to the world, seeking desperately needed western capital, technology, and management skills. For their part, western businesses see potentially enormous untapped markets, a land rich in resources, and an educated work force. But they are also overwhelmed by an absence of clear, concise, stable laws governing western investment. In fact, the current Soviet business legislation is one of the most severe barriers to western investment. The most glaring testimony to the impediments created by the confusing checkerboard of twenty-plus decrees and laws is the fact that fewer than than 10 percent of the 1,500 to 2,000 joint venture agreements signed since the 1987 joint venture law was enacted are even marginally operational. To make matters worse, the slow emergence of competitive commercial banking, commercial credit, and indigenous capital markets—fundamental prerequisites to a viable, market-oriented private

sector—renders impossible the most routine financial intermediation.

This volume opens with the three seminar working groups'
findings and recommendations. In the view of the Soviet and
western participants, reawakening the slumbering, decaying
Soviet economy is impossible without the privatization of property
and significant headway in three critical areas: business law,
money and banking, and capital markets.

BUSINESS LAW

The Soviet Union desperately needs management, marketing, and
technological skills from the West if it is to compete in the world
economy. However, development of joint ventures and western
business in general has been slowed by the lack of clear legal
business guidelines.

The business law working group's recommendations spring
from a careful assessment of the Soviet Ministry of Justice's March
1990 draft joint venture law and more generally from the elements needed for a comprehensive business code. Reforms must be
"comprehensive and radical, not piecemeal and cautious," the
group reports. The Soviet Union should consider adopting existing
western business codes, such as the German code, which is already
the basis of its civil code, and other widely accepted international
conventions, such as those on copyright and the international sale
of goods.

A six-member team of western and Soviet legal specialists acted
upon the group's recommendations, and in August 1990 they produced the first bilaterally authored draft law on foreign investment
for the Russian Federation. The law covers joint-stock companies
(with up to 100 percent ownership), joint ventures, the operation of
foreign business in the Soviet Union, and the creation and operation of special trade zones. As of this writing, Vice President
Ruslan Khasbulatov has approved the Geonomics draft in principle,
and it has been introduced for deliberation and possible enactment
by the Russian Parliament.[1]

---

1. The draft law appears in Part III of this volume.

MONEY AND BANKING

A market economy requires a diverse and well-developed banking system to gather funds, pay realistic interest rates to savers, and lend to qualified borrowers for home, business, and consumer needs. The Soviet banking system has not had to fulfill any of these roles. State banks simply funneled money to state enterprises based on centrally planned directives and goals. With little to buy, consumers were forced to save regardless of the real rate of return.

The recent development of independent commercial banks is a start toward creating a diversified and market-oriented banking system, but much remains to be done. The money and banking working group offers six recommendations to create a stable, market-oriented banking system and to encourage voluntary saving and investment.

CAPITAL MARKETS

The Soviet Union will ultimately need some form of a securities and bond market as state monopolies are converted to privately owned firms and as the government issues bonds for capital projects and to finance its growing budget deficits. Current political and economic uncertainties, as well as past ideological opposition to private property and stock ownership, will undoubtedly impede the development of capital markets. However, the working group concluded that capital markets can be phased in beginning with state-issued, gold-backed bonds and with municipal bonds for capital improvements.

Part I of this volume includes the working group reports. Part II opens with chapter 4 by Josef C. Brada. Brada offers an analysis of the economic, legal, and political difficulties that the Soviet Union and East Europe will face in expanding trade with the West. After years of self-imposed economic isolation, issues from repatriation of profits to the determination of fair export prices for heavily subsidized goods will assuredly pose problems.

Unfortunately, there are no international institutions equipped to deal with the range and scope of issues. The World Bank, the

International Monetary Fund, and the General Agreement on Tariffs and Trade were designed to promote development and to regulate trade among market-oriented economies. The Council on Mutual Economic Assistance, the Soviet-dominated organization of centrally planned economies, is similarly able to confront issues indigenous to the East Bloc and its members' inconvertible currencies. Brada concludes that new mechanisms are needed to help create standards, exchange views, and reconcile differing interests during this transitional period. Such institutions would bridge the gap until countries could qualify for full membership in western international institutions.

In chapter 5, Vladimir T. Musatov explores institutional reforms effected under perestroika to date, particularly those in financial activities. His paper provocatively claims that, properly understood, the Soviet system was already a market economy, albeit a distorted one, prior to 1985.

Peter J. Pettibone in chapter 6 assumes the position that U.S. policy toward the Soviet Union places American business leaders at a distinct disadvantage in their commercial transactions while also significantly hampering the prospects for an early return of the Soviet Union to the world economy. Pettibone also offers a series of specific actions the administration and Congress can take to improve Soviet-U.S. trade relations.

According to Francis A. Scotland in chapter 7, central planning and the use of money as an administrative tool rather than as a means of economic allocation have provided macroeconomic stability, but at the cost of severely constraining Soviet economic progress. Market-based financial reform, complete with proper checks and balances, he maintains, can help rejuvenate growth and achieve a higher standard of living for all Soviets. Scotland proposes a series of specific financial market reforms, several of which break new ground in the reform debate.

In chapter 8, John A. Bohn, Jr. and David H. Levey analyze the appropriate institutional structure and the proper procedures to accomplish credit risk analysis in the Soviet Union. From the perspective of Moody's Investors Service, for which they work, Bohn and Levey argue that privatization, price reform, and the elimination of soft enterprise budget constraints are the fundamental preconditions of the development of any form of credit risk analysis in the Soviet system. Against this backdrop it is argued that a transition to the universal banking systems employed by much of continental Europe, wherein financing is provided by large banks within a tightly knit oligopoly, is the most likely in the Soviet case. Indeed, the Bohn-Levey thesis is quite consistent with the arguments proffered by Francis Scotland in the previous chapter.

Bohn and Levey believe that a valuable role exists for an independent rating agency like Moody's in fostering the Soviet Union's capital markets. Ratings provide a quick, convenient means of communicating credit opinions to the marketplace. Rating agencies also develop industry-based databases that can be used to generate publicly available financial information. As such, ratings have significant value to bankers, capital market regulators, and issuers of debt, as well as to investors.

In chapter 9, Keith A. Rosten provides a sometimes surprising survey of the problems, challenges, and opportunities faced by those entering into joint ventures with Soviet partners. His paper provides one of the few available inside accounts of the process of organizing and operating a business on Soviet soil. After reporting and interpreting his survey results in some detail, Rosten extracts a series of practical and concrete recommendations to those contemplating pioneering in the nascent stage of Soviet-U.S. joint venture development.

Senior legal scholar Viktor P. Mozolin offers in chapter 10 a Soviet view of the reform process and the legal reform that should accompany social and economic reform. Mozolin argues for radical legal reforms, under which all laws intended to ensure the functioning of the centrally planned economy must be renounced. Problems notwithstanding, successful radical legal reform must come before economic legislation. Mozolin seeks a system of general and coordinated laws concerning the management of the economy that would obviate the need for an internationally unusual separate law regulating joint ventures. Following the presentation of his paper at the Geonomics conference, Mozolin was largely successful in exhorting his business law working group to call for the complete overhaul of Soviet business law.

Peter B. Maggs, America's leading legal scholar on Soviet matters, echoes Mozolin by arguing in chapter 11 that changes in the general legal system, not in specific provisions of joint venture legislation, have the greater long-run impact on the legal climate within which joint ventures must operate. The current system fails to provide minimum legal guarantees necessary for the proper operation of a market economy. Soviet business legislation has been unstable, unpredictable, and largely unpublished since 1988, a situation that impacts negatively in establishing and operating joint ventures. Maggs reiterates Mozolin's call for a universal law governing business operations, and he specifically calls for an immediate end to price regulation, antimonopoly legislation, greater flexibility in organizational structure, and, most importantly, transition from a discretionary to a declaratory system for creating enterprises.

Alexander L. Katkov asks a potentially much more disturbing question in chapter 12: Can joint ventures help to create a market economy in the Soviet Union? The key reform issue, as he sees it, is the privatization of state-owned enterprises. Katkov argues that it is possible to use joint ventures as a key element in designing a new market-oriented Soviet economy that has regained a deep involvement in the global economy. However, the joint venture should be but one component of a much more comprehensive program. Katkov supports creating free trade zones and stock, bond, and commodity markets, calls for placing a higher priority on achieving a convertible ruble, and lobbies the United States to dismantle its anti-Soviet, Cold War legislation. To motivate foreign investors to move capital into the Soviet Union, Katkov endorses eliminating all barriers to foreign investment, enacting a reasonable tax policy, and shielding against political risk in the form of a declaration of the state's responsibility to provide a guarantee of compensation of foreign investment.

Michail A. Portnoy states in chapter 13 that financing is one of the primary problems western partners face when they try to establish joint ventures. The virtual independence of joint ventures (compared to Soviet enterprises), and the lack of experience in dealing with them, has made Soviet banks so cautious as to erect often fatal financing barriers to their establishment and operation. Portnoy also discusses in some detail a host of other institutional hurdles faced by western business leaders participating in joint ventures.

In the summer of 1990, Geonomics convened a workshop to take up the recommendations of the May seminar's business law working group. Following Viktor P. Mozolin's arrival carrying a personal request from Russian Federation President Boris Yeltsin, the group of six western and Soviet lawyers, economists, and business leaders accepted the challenge to draft a new law on foreign investment for the Russian Republic. The March 1990 Soviet Ministry of Justice draft joint venture law appears in Part III of this volume, which also includes Keith A. Rosten's survey of reasons motivating the effort to create new business laws for the Soviet Union.

On August 3, 1990, the Geonomics Institute released the workshop's draft law on foreign investment for the Russian Republic. It was subsequently delivered to President Yeltsin and his vice president, Ruslan Khasbulatov, in September. Following their review and approval of the draft in principle, it was introduced into the Russian Parliament for consideration and possible enactment.

Josef C. Brada
Michael P. Claudon

Part I

Working Group Proposals

1

Working Group 1:
Business Law

Viktor P. Mozolin and Peter J. Pettibone

In the three-plus years since the Presidium of the Supreme Soviet passed decrees permitting joint ventures, over 1,400 agreements have been signed. But the initial high hopes of western partners, interested in gaining access to a market of 280 million and to pockets of Soviet technological expertise, and Soviet enterprise managers, interested in the technology, management, and marketing skills of the West, have rarely been realized.

Less than 10 percent of the joint ventures are operational. Most of those ventures are in services, and many are simply legalized export-import operations. More complex high-technology ventures, so necessary in the modernization of the Soviet economy, have frequently not progressed beyond the talking stage.

There have been many reasons for this: an inadequate Soviet infrastructure, from roads to communications to available office space; unrealistic, "planned" prices that often bear no relation to costs; an inconvertible ruble that makes repatriation of profits into dollars very difficult; and lack of a common business culture.

Another major problem is the lack of clear legal guidelines on the establishment and operation of joint ventures. Since 1988, legislation on joint ventures and on the Soviet economy has often been unstable, unpredictable, and largely unpublished. Unlike in the West, where the creation of a corporation is relatively simple, fast, and inexpensive, approval of joint ventures in the Soviet Union appears to depend on a combination of written rules, unwritten rules,

11

officials' discretion, and support of influential persons. In essence, Soviet bureaucrats regard issuance of a corporate charter as a privilege rather than a right. Initial negotiating and legal costs of $100,000 and upwards have been a major barrier to small, innovative, high-technology western companies.

If joint ventures are to succeed, there must be a legal culture that enables potential investors to know their rights and obligations. New laws, such as the Ownership Law, are providing more flexibility in the creation of joint ventures, but there are many unresolved areas. Current Soviet law, for example, is unclear on the protection of "intellectual property," inventions, and trade secrets—all important considerations for high-technology companies. Western companies also need clearer legislation on land rights before they will build on Soviet soil. Foreign partners can obtain land as part of the Soviet partner's contribution or by leasing, but it has been very difficult for foreigners to determine the legality of the lease or partner's contribution.

Complicating the resolution of these legal issues is a severe shortage of westerners with a knowledge of the Soviet legal system and experience in the Soviet Union. Similarly, there are almost no experienced Soviet private law firms involved in international business law. Administrative rulemaking generally proceeds with little opportunity for comment from interested parties. Furthermore, many Soviet administrative regulations are unpublished and inaccessible. There are no commercial courts and no arbitration bodies that draw on arbitrators from an international pool of specialists.

If joint ventures and ultimately western business investment are to flourish, a clear, comprehensive business code is essential. In the following report, workshop participants, including Soviet and western specialists in business law, have developed a series of recommendations on the draft of a revised joint venture law and for the essentials in a comprehensive business code.

Just as reforming the Soviet economy and integrating it into the world economy is an enormous challenge, so is the challenge of developing an appropriate legal system. The task is complex, but the rewards for East and West demand that we go forward.

RECOMMENDATIONS

Basic Assumptions

The long-term goal of this legislative reform is to help change the Soviet economic system into a market economy and to facilitate greater East-West business and joint ventures.

General Recommendations

1. Legislative reform should be comprehensive and radical, not piecemeal and cautious. Legislative reform will not work if it proceeds slowly.
2. New laws should integrate with the existing civil code system. Since the Civil Code of the Russian Federation is based mainly on the civil codes of Germany, it would be appropriate for the Soviet Union to study the bankruptcy, secured transactions, and other laws in Germany, France, Switzerland, and other West European civil law countries to determine how those laws are integrated into their legal systems. (It is not an affront to the sovereignty of the Soviet Union for it to borrow in their entirety laws of other countries. Adopting whole laws should avoid inconsistencies inherent in a piecemeal approach.)
3. Because the Supreme Soviet is unlikely to adopt legislative reform that is both comprehensive and radical given the great differences of opinion on that subject within that body, we suggest that the republics (and perhaps other governmental bodies) be given the right to enact legislation in the business sphere and that business organizations organized under those laws be permitted to engage in business transactions under the authority of those laws anywhere within the Soviet Union.
4. The Soviet Union should accede to widely accepted international business conventions such as the Berne Convention (copyright) and the Vienna Convention (international sale of goods).

Specific Legislative Proposals

1. A comprehensive, integrated business organizations law, which would permit joint-stock companies (with up to 100 percent foreign ownership), joint ventures, and other forms of general and limited liability organizations.
2. Comprehensive laws regulating secured transactions that authorize mortgages/security interests on (1) land and buildings, (2) movable capital goods (for example, aircraft and ships), and (3) accounts receivable and other intangibles, and that provide for the registration of mortgages/security interests on movable and immovable property.
3. A bankruptcy law.
4. Tax laws that are simple in operation, broad in application, and have relatively low rates.
5. A new patent law (a second draft has been prepared).
6. A trade secret/know-how law.
7. Antimonopoly laws, including repealing laws restricting joint ventures from engaging in specific activities, for example, the specific activity of insurance.
8. "Safety net" social legislation.
9. Repeal the laws setting and regulating prices.

2

Working Group 2: Money and Banking

Michail Alekseev and William Orr

Since the beginning of perestroika in 1987, the Soviet banking system has passed through the first phase of reform. At the time of this workshop, the Soviet government is considering a second phase of reform, which is to include changes that will take effect in both the short and long terms.

The current banking system has two classes of banks: those run by the government and those run by private parties (enterprises and cooperatives, not individuals). At the head of the government banks is Gosbank, the Soviet state bank. It supervises and controls five specialized banks:

- *Agroprombank* for agriculture
- *Zhilsotsbank* for municipal services
- *Promstroi* bank for industrial construction
- *Sberbank* for personal savings
- *Vnesheconombank* for international banking

The specialized banks were set up to loan exclusively in their own economic sectors, but now they can make loans in one another's sectors.

The independent, or commercial, banking system consists of:

- Branch banks created by large enterprises
- Cooperative banks to finance cooperative enterprises
- Innovation banks to finance new ventures

15

The number of commercial banks is growing rapidly. At the latest report there were 265, with more than 60 in Moscow. Participants in the banking workshop strongly and unanimously agreed that establishment of a stable, market-oriented banking system is essential for the growth of a market economy in the Soviet Union and for integrating that economy into the global financial system. However, the participants felt that it might be disastrously counterproductive if all of the recommended reforms were implemented at once, because any banking system tends to be an amplifier of financial imbalances. We therefore recommend that some measures be deferred while the financial system is still unstable due to fiscal and price reforms, removal of state subsidies, and widespread bankruptcies. We feel that our first, and most seminal, recommendation should be implemented immediately: Designate Gosbank as the central bank and make it totally independent of the government. The central bank should have clearly defined areas of responsibility and the firm understanding that it should be free to meet its responsibilities without political intervention. The recommendations aimed at building a sound infrastructure for the future commercial banking system should also begin at once. Our model here is the announcement of "EC 1992," the creation of an integrated European market, years before its implementation date. This kind of groundwork focuses interests and energies and maps the direction for a common effort. We recommend that the Soviet government work toward the following six major goals. We also invite attention to certain implementation tasks.

RECOMMENDATIONS

I.   Set Up a Central Bank with Independent Powers to:

- Control the money supply
- Assure the security of the credit system
- Regulate and supervise the commercial banking system

1. The central bank should have an operating charter that is free of political influence.

2. The independence of the central bank should be enhanced by making the terms of its governors longer than those of People's Deputies and staggered so as not to coincide with elections.
3. The central bank should not be required to purchase government bonds issued to finance its debt.
4. Some kind of insurance should be provided for depositors against the failure of commercial banks. The system should have built-in protection ("fire walls") to assure that depositor insurance is not used to transfer risk from nonfinancial operations to the financial operations of commercial banks.
5. Commercial banks should be required to keep reserves on deposit in the central bank.
6. The central bank should have the power to suspend activities of noncomplying banks.

II. **The Government Should Enable and Encourage Growth of a Competitive Banking Industry.**

1. Commercial banks should be able to accept the deposits of individuals and institutions.
2. Commercial banks should have tax incentives to introduce new banking technologies.
3. Commercial banks should be able to underwrite bonds and sell stock shares.
4. At the appropriate time, commercial banks should be able to make consumer loans to individuals.
5. Commercial banks should be subject to the discipline of possible bankruptcy.
6. The government should study the desirability of enabling financial institutions to secure classes of loans and sell them on a secondary market.
7. Commercial banks should not be burdened with losses arising from past reforms, that is, from the elimination of price distortions.
8. The government should provide for correspondent banking services to increase efficiency by lowering overhead costs.

III. Adopt Measures to Encourage Voluntary Saving and Investment.

1. Encourage creation of a money market with a variety of debt instruments and interest rates (for example, different interest rates for different loan maturities, a provision that should be enacted during the financial transition).
2. Exempt from income taxes the interest on savings.
3. Create pension, retirement, and mutual investment funds to encourage long-term savings.
4. Enable payment in advance for scarce consumer goods, such as autos, refrigerators, and houses.
5. Enable Soviet citizens to deposit foreign exchange in Soviet banks. Grant amnesty to activities that in the past may have been illegal, in order to place hard currency under government control and discourage black-market operations in foreign exchange.
6. Enable the leasing of equipment and services to stimulate innovation.

IV. Adopt Measures to Manage the Public Debt.

1. Issue a variety of government notes and bonds with a variety of maturities, with market rates set by auction.
2. Enable local governments to issue bonds at market rates.
3. Exempt from income taxes the interest on central government and local government bonds.
4. Provide a secondary market that will enable individuals to own government bonds.

V. Link Soviet Banking to the International Financial System.

1. Create favorable conditions for foreign banks to operate in the Soviet Union.
2. Adopt measures to protect foreign investments placed in the Soviet Union.

3. Enable foreign banks established in the Soviet Union to provide services that compete with Soviet banks in various areas.
4. Move toward membership in international financial bodies such as the International Monetary Fund (IMF), the World Bank, the General Agreement on Tariffs and Trade (GATT), and the Organization of Economic Cooperation and Development (OECD).

VI. Immediately Plan, Announce, and Take Steps to Build a Modern Infrastructure for the Future Banking System.

1. Adopt and announce a timetable for enacting legislative measures enabling a free-market banking system.
2. Computerize banking operations wherever possible and as soon as possible to make them competitive and compatible with operations of advanced market economies.
3. Meet IMF formats and standards in publishing aggregate information on such macroeconomic indicators as banking activity, various categories of savings, production, money supply, interest rates, and inflation. The data should be published by the central bank to assure acceptance of their impartiality.
4. Require detailed disclosures in prospectuses, reports to the government, and reports to shareholders.
5. Encourage independent analyses and ratings of financial risks.
6. Study common western practices in acquiring, calculating, and publishing statistical information.
7. Immediately remove the present ceilings on salaries paid to state bank employees.
8. Encourage professional auditing of commercial banks by western accounting firms.
9. Encourage the training of Soviet finance personnel in western methods in high schools and universities, through translation of important foreign documents into Russian, and in a broad range of other ways.
10. Launch long-term, broad public-education programs to quickly raise the general level of understanding of banking and financial matters.

3

Working Group 3: Capital Markets

Vladimir T. Musatov, John A. Bohn, Jr., and David H. Levey

The Soviet Union has a full and controversial plate of economic programs and proposals as it attempts to modernize and convert its centrally planned economy to some form of a free-market system. Soviet and western economic advisers believe that development of a capital and securities market will play several important roles in these reforms, including:

1. The government now owns and largely controls the output of more than 90 percent of the country's industrial base. Transforming these state monopolies into private, joint-stock companies would give the firms autonomy from central control and state investment and force them to become more efficient. Very simply, in order to attract new investment from independent investors, the firms would have to offer competitive and higher-quality goods to create shareholder value and consumer interest.

2. Workers would have alternative and potentially more lucrative outlets for their savings. State banks currently pay interest rates well below the inflation rate. Purchase of shares could help reduce the inflationary pressure from the billions of rubles that are involuntarily held in savings banks because of widespread consumer goods shortages.

3. Shares could also provide much-needed incentives for workers to become more involved in their work.

4. True capital markets could help fund a new entrepreneurial class that would bring needed consumer and high-technology goods to the market.

While the Soviet Union is currently preparing legislation creating joint-stock companies, the country faces enormous problems in creating an active capital market. Central planning and widespread state subsidies have created a pricing system that often bears little relation to true costs. How, for example, can the worth of a firm be evaluated when it is viable only with state subsidies? As many as one-fifth of state enterprises may be technically bankrupt and many more could not survive in a competitive environment. Many state monopolies are simply not very attractive investments, according to western and Soviet observers.

Widespread economic instability—inflation, unrealistic exchange and interest rates, budget deficits, frequent economic policy shifts, lack of clarity on ownership of private property—does not create favorable conditions for long-term investments. Until there is greater stability and agreement on economic reforms, development of capital markets is likely to be slow.

Not since Czarist rule at the turn of the century has the country had a stock exchange. Creating trust and investor interest in a stock exchange will also take time in a country where confiscation of wealth remains a real fear.

Aside from these larger economic preconditions, there are many technical questions to be answered. What, for example, will be the role of banks in the development of bond and stock markets? In the United States, bond and stock issues cannot, by law, be handled by commercial and savings banks. In order to reduce risk, autonomous investment banks and corporations issue bonds and stocks. Institutional and individual investors rely on independent advisory services and ratings, along with extensive disclosure from firms, in making investment decisions.

Most of the conditions for a U.S.-type system do not exist in the Soviet Union. The universal banking system of much of continental Europe is closer to the Soviet system and is likely to be the model for its development. Under universal banking, large, oligopolistic banks can oversee bond and stock issues. Independent credit analysis and disclosure of company information are much more limited. But defaults are very rare because of the close bank and corporate ties.

In developing its recommendations, the working group assumed that the Soviet Union, given its highly centralized banking system, would adopt the universal banking approach. For the purpose of this study, we adopted a western legal framework and its definitions and laws on corporations, equity, and debt.

Given the complexity of existing problems, the group recommends that the Soviet Union begin development of capital markets with the state's issuance of gold-backed bonds directed to large institutional investors such as commercial banks. We also proposed three ways of converting state enterprises into private firms. Privatization will be a difficult and delicate process and requires much further study.

RECOMMENDATIONS

The purpose of the working group was to make some recommendations for the development of financial markets in the Soviet Union. Before we could do that, however, we felt that there must first exist a legal framework that provides the basic rules, definitions, and laws on corporations, equity, and debt. With this in mind, we adopted, for the purposes of this study, western definitions of what a corporation is, what a share is, what the rights and privileges of a shareholder are, and what the rights and privileges of an issuer are.

The best place for the Soviet Union to start building a financial market is at the state level with issuance of zero-coupon gold-backed bonds. These bonds should be long-term, high-denomination instruments directed toward the institutional investor, that is, commercial banks and enterprises. Such bonds could also be sold to individual investors but the denomination makes this unlikely.

Subsequently, municipal bonds should be issued to the general public with the restriction that they be used for capital improvements only. We feel that these bonds are the most promising means for building the Soviet infrastructure and will be very popular with the public. Municipalities should issue these bonds at low rates.

Corporate bonds should be issued with a consumer-good component in the form of a warrant or coupon redeemable upon maturity. We can call these instruments enterprise bonds.

We offer two alternatives for the privatization of the industrial sector, both of which must be explored in further detail:

1. Equity shares will be given to the employees of industrial enterprises in equal proportions. A percent of the total equity of each firm will be placed in a state-administered mutual fund to be divided equally among all individuals that work outside of the industrial sector. Equities will not be allowed to be traded outside of the firm for an initial period of two to five years. Once this period expires, these issues can be freely traded on any of the regional exchanges (discussed below).

2. A large portion of the corporation's equity will be held by the corporation to be exchanged with other industrial firms. The remaining equity will be distributed among corporate employees following employee stock ownership plan guidelines.

We expect regional exchanges to be established in each republic. These exchanges should be linked electronically and regulated from a central body developed at the state level.

Instruments:
- Gold-backed state bonds
- Municipal bonds
- Corporate bonds with consumer-goods warrants
- Common stock
- State-run municipal fund
- No preferred stock

Mechanisms:
- Commercial banks
- Regional stock exchanges
- Regulatory body

Part II

Analyzing the Issues

4

Integrating the Soviet Union and East Europe into the World Economy: A Call for New Institutions

Josef C. Brada

INTRODUCTION

At the same time that many West European countries are moving confidently toward 1992, the economies of the Soviet Union and East Europe are moving, with much less confidence and certainty but with at least as much hope, toward a new economic future. While the specific means of achieving this new future are as yet unclear, the broad outlines of their goals and means of reaching them may be discerned. The Soviet Union and East European countries seek to achieve more productive and prosperous economies by means of a greater reliance on markets and private property as well as through greater trade with the West. These developments in the two parts of Europe interact with each other in various ways. In the realm of economics, it is clear that the trade of the Soviet Union and East Europe will be reoriented toward the West, and that the flows of capital, technology, and business know-how between the two parts of Europe will increase.

While such an increase in East-West trade and investment should have positive effects, the ability of governments to influence the distribution of these benefits and to manage the social and political consequences of these expanded economic contacts needs to be examined. Currently, East-West relations are evolving in a variety of ways: through bilateral country-to-country contacts; through relations between individual countries and international organizations such as the General Agreement on Tariffs and Trade (GATT);

and through relations between individual countries and supernational organizations such as the EC, and within regional integration blocs such as the EC, the EFTA, and the CMEA. However, most of these organizations were formed at a different time and for different purposes. In general, these organizations were set up to achieve the objectives of groups of like-minded countries with similar economic systems. Whether organizations constituted in this way will be able to deal effectively with the problems of countries transitioning from state planning and social ownership to a more market-oriented system is doubtful. The fact that most of these organizations were formed in ways that did not span across capitalist and socialist economic systems suggests that their ability to serve as a bridge between East and West in this period of rapid economic, political, and social change needs to be examined with some care, and if present organizations are found to be lacking, then thought must be given to creating new ones.

THE ECONOMIC LANDSCAPE IN EAST EUROPE: A GUESS

At this time, the Soviet Union and the countries of East Europe differ in their conceptions of the objectives of economic reforms and in the pace at which they wish to implement these reforms. Some, such as Czechoslovakia, Hungary, and Poland, appear to be aiming at the creation of systems where markets and the role of private property predominate. Other countries—for example, the Soviet Union, Bulgaria, and Romania—have not entirely abandoned directive planning as the principal means of allocating resources, and the role of private production continues to be seen as an auxiliary rather than dominant form of business organization. Nevertheless, starting as they are from economic systems where state ownership is virtually all-encompassing in industry, where market forces have been subjugated to directive plans, where relative prices are far from equilibrium, and where a great number of the institutions that are necessary for the functioning of a capitalist market economy are only now being constructed, it is important to conceive of how they should be organized and how they will function.

Ownership of the Means of Production

Privatization will proceed slowly whatever the intention of policy-makers. This is principally due to the fact that in none of these countries is there a desire to simply hand over ownership to the population by means of some sort of social distribution of property rights. In Czechoslovakia, Hungary, and Poland, thinking about privatization has proceeded the farthest. State-owned enterprises are to be turned into joint-stock companies whose shares will at first be held by a state property office, or by institutions such as pension funds or banks. Subsequently or simultaneously, these shares will also be made available to residents of these countries, to the companies' workers at favorable prices or through employee stock ownership plans (ESOPs), and to foreign buyers. However, domestic savings are a fraction of the book value of industrial capital, and there exists no domestic financial system capable of providing residents with the credit needed to purchase state-owned assets. Schemes to supplement the purchasing power of the population by issuing vouchers redeemable for shares in companies are, at least in Poland, where the program is in its most concrete form, relatively modest.

Generalizations in the Soviet Union are more difficult because the pace and nature of reform varies greatly from republic to republic. In the Baltic Republics, for example, extensive privatization is contemplated, though there, too, the obstacles to its implementation are similar to those encountered in East Europe. In other republics, most notably the Russian Soviet Federated Socialist Republic, by far the largest element of the Soviet economy, the creation of corporations is also envisioned, but privatization, at least for now, will consist only of sales of stock to foreigners. Finally, no movement toward privatization of large-scale industry is evident at this time in Romania and Bulgaria.

These practical and political barriers to privatization suggest that, in both the more reformist as well as in the less reform-minded economies, there will continue to be a large state-owned sector in industry, managed by some combination of state-appointed managers and workers' councils and by managers who will lease and operate state-owned property. The state sector will coexist and compete with private firms that have been purchased by foreign firms, by domestic financial institutions, and by home-country residents. In addition, there will be privatization from below, as the formation of mainly small, private businesses is allowed. These natural barriers to a rapid privatization of the capital stock will be augmented by widely shared perceptions that communications, transportation, public utilities, and other public services should remain in state hands.

Markets and Prices

The distorted nature of relative prices and monetary disequilibria have made reformers cautious about price reform. Too rapid a freeing of prices is seen as being fraught with danger. In part this is because reformers are pessimistic about the downward flexibility of prices, believing that even relative price changes would have an inflationary impact, while the existence of pent-up purchasing power is seen as a barrier to price flexibility in all countries save Poland. Moreover, to the extent that prices are flexible downward, a too rapid realignment carries with it the danger of unacceptable levels of unemployment. Thus, both the desire to limit the pace and range of relative price changes and the distortion by inflationary forces of the information conveyed by prices suggest that markets will not, over the course of the transition, provide the quantity or type of information available in developed market economies.

Money and Capital Markets

Probably the least effective but most important markets will be those for capital. While most reforms call for converting state enterprises into joint-stock companies, this in itself will not guarantee the creation of efficient equity or credit markets. The newly formed joint-stock companies will be closely held, either by the government, by a small group of commercial banks, by specially organized holding companies, by worker ESOPs, or by foreigners. Each of these owners will tend to hold large blocs of shares and will have little interest in, or, in the case of ESOPs, ability to, trade shares actively on the market. Thus, the obstacles to valuing the shares of these firms through an efficient equities market will be similar to those encountered in the valuation of the stock of closely held firms in market economies.

The changeover from a socialist accounting system whose main purpose was to monitor enterprise compliance with central plans to one designed to value financial and resource flows and stocks on the basis of market prices will create a great deal of confusion. Profit and loss and the value of assets will change not only as prices are freed, but also as fundamental accounting concepts are altered, even as the terminology remains the same. The lack of trained accountants and of auditors will also raise questions regarding the quality of information on the economic performance of firms.

To regulate the supply of credit, Hungary and Czechoslovakia have created a network of commercial banks in the hope that these will impose financial discipline on firms seeking loans. Unfortunately, these commercial banks have been saddled with the outstanding loans of existing state enterprises. Many of these loans were issued at the behest of planners on the basis of criteria other than profitability at either past or prospective prices, and consequently many of them are likely to cause problems for enterprises and banks alike. Thus, both the supply of bank credit and the terms under which it is available may not fully reflect market conditions.

At the same time, the pressure on capital markets will be intense. The volume of investment will probably fall as consumers will be able to compete for goods more effectively than they could in the past when the enterprise sector operated on a soft budget constraint. Also at the same time, important capital allocation decisions will have to be made. In part, there will be a need for difficult capital allocation decisions due to the need to restructure and reduce the bloated industrial structures of these countries. Which firms or, given the size of firms in these countries, which sectors of industry are to be eliminated and which are to survive will have to be decided relatively quickly. Foreign trade will be reallocated toward the West, and thus at the same time that some sectors of industry are being eliminated, others will require new infusions of capital and technology in order to compete in western markets. Emerging private firms are likely to be undercapitalized and thus will have a strong demand for credit, particularly if this sector experiences a rapid growth in demand. Lending to these firms, however, will be risky, both because of their fragile financial foundations and the inexperience of their owners.

In sum, in even the most reform-minded of the economies of East Europe, the role of the state as an allocator of resources, and especially of investment resources, as well as an owner of industrial enterprises will remain an important if not dominant feature of the economic mechanism. At the same time, market generated signals will be weak, will contain much noise, and will be subject to considerable misinterpretation by economic agents unaccustomed to functioning in a market environment. In economies where less radical reforms are envisioned, the weakness of market signals, of course, will be even greater and the role of the state correspondingly stronger.

EAST-WEST TRADE AND EXISTING INSTITUTIONS

In the West, a number of international and supernational organizations have evolved to promote commerce among market economies. Once it is accepted that the economies of the East cannot be transformed rapidly into market economies with extensive private ownership, the ability of these organizations to facilitate the expansion of East-West trade and investment becomes doubtful. This is primarily because these international organizations have developed rules that, while appropriate and adequate for promoting commerce among market economies, are likely to be inadequate or counterproductive for facilitating and mediating East-West trade.

Reducing Trade Barriers and Increasing Economic Integration

The principal means for reducing tariffs and other barriers to trade among the market economies has been the GATT. The GATT's ability to reduce trade barriers rests on the willingness of its members to grant one another reciprocal nondiscriminatory treatment on tariffs and other trade barriers and to negotiate periodically multilateral reductions in tariffs. Such an emphasis on tariff reductions as a means of promoting trade is unlikely to be of much use in the case of countries where trade will be carried out largely by state firms or agencies in an environment characterized by seriously distorted prices. Indeed, as these countries liberalize their systems and as prices assume a greater role, the level of tariffs may need to be increased to prevent domestic price distortions from spilling over into incorrect and destabilizing trade and investment flows.

The inability of the GATT mechanism to deal adequately with the problems of East-West trade is amply demonstrated by the general dissatisfaction of the GATT's members with the conditions under which Poland, Romania, and Hungary joined the organization. Even the reform measures of the East European countries, with the possible exception of the Polish reform, are unlikely to improve their compatibility with GATT principles because state trading will remain the dominant way in which these countries will participate in international trade. The GATT has had great difficulty in dealing with state trading by market economies, with no general principles having evolved to mediate conflicts among members. Indeed, the GATT's efforts to generate principles to liberalize the state trading practices of East Europe are likely to be caught up in, and be held up by, conflicts among the market economies over state trading among themselves in telecommunications and other strategic sectors. Thus, solutions applicable to East Europe may be blocked because of their implications for the resolution of West-West conflicts over state trade, or solutions to West-West conflicts on state trading may be carried over to East-West trade with little regard for their suitability.

East-West trade liberalization could be freed from both the inappropriate GATT criterion of nondiscriminatory tariff treatment and the contentiousness of West-West state trading conflicts by establishing an organization whose exclusive task would be limited to regulating and liberalizing East-West trade. All interested East European countries and western countries would be free to belong.

For the Soviet Union and the East European countries, a special standard of nondiscrimination against the West would be appropriate. To deal with the state trading practices of the East, something more than nondiscriminatory tariff treatment would be required. Thus, standards for the transparency and nondiscriminatory nature of the decisions of state trading agencies, of taxes and subsidies for state enterprises, and of these countries' commercial policies would have to be negotiated by the members of the new organization and adhered to by those members whose trade is carried out by state trading companies. This would also provide assurance to western countries that their exports to the East were competing on a level playing field and would reduce western concerns over dumping. Issues such as controls over technology exports and determination of market disruption could also be resolved by such an organization. The expansion of East-West trade and the establishment of means for resolving, if not avoiding, East-West trade problems could thus proceed within this new organization without having to bend and adapt inapplicable GATT principles, without creating precedents for dealing with West-West state trading within the GATT, and without embroiling East-West conflicts over state trading in conflicts over state trading among western economies.

The creation of an international organization to facilitate the expansion of East-West trade would also reduce the likelihood that the East European countries and the Soviet Union will place undue reliance on the European Community (EC) or the European Free Trade Area (EFTA) as a vehicle for their reintegration into the world trading system. Although trade with West Europe, and thus with these two integration schemes, will play a pivotal role in the expansion of East European trade with the West, the East European countries are many years away from being viable candidates for membership in either the EC or the EFTA. While a close form of associate status or special relationship with the EC is possible for some East European countries, the development of such bloc to bloc special relations would come at the expense of East European trade with the United States, Japan, and the non-EC countries of West Europe. Such an economic predominance of the EC in East Europe would likely create political and economic strains between the EC and other western countries, a consideration further confirming the need for and the desirability of a multilateral approach to the expansion of East-West trade.

Financing Trade and Capital Flows

The International Monetary Fund's operating principle of currency convertibility is, of course, met only by a minority of its members. Nevertheless, the simultaneous introduction of a large group of relatively developed countries with inconvertible currencies and serious payments and debt problems into the IMF may prove disruptive to the organization. Moreover, the IMF's emphasis on convertibility, its credit facilities, and its large membership do not make it a particularly useful vehicle for facilitating the liberalization of payments between East and West and particularly not for facilitating the liberalization of payments among the countries of East Europe. These intra-CMEA trade flows, often based on correct perceptions of comparative advantage and supported by years of contacts between trading partners, can play a valuable role in East Europe's development if they can be freed from the bilateralism imposed by the inconvertibility of the currencies of the East European countries.

Thus, a clearing bank along the lines of the IMF, but whose membership consisted of the interested East European countries, the Soviet Union, and the developed western countries, could facilitate clearing of payments in both East-West and East-East arrangements. Members would contribute national currencies, which would be available for lending to other members. By employing a mix of convertible western and inconvertible eastern currencies in the clearing and lending operations of the bank, the eastern currencies would achieve a degree of acceptability in international settlements that could not be achieved in intra-CMEA clearing operations. Limits would be placed on each country's ability to draw down the bank's hard currency holdings, which would encourage clearing and borrowing in eastern currencies while providing East European governments at least a limited ability to convert holdings of inconvertible East European currencies into convertible western currencies.

Long-Term Lending for Economic Development

East Europe and the Soviet Union will need investment in infrastructure, including communications and transportation, if they are to succeed in their efforts to expand trade with the West. At the same time, there will be significant investment needs as East European industries are restructured in response to signals from the world market. Some East European countries, such as Hungary and Romania, belong to the World Bank, which provides long-term and concessionary loans precisely for such developmental programs. However, the countries of East Europe are not developing countries. Despite their current economic travails, neither their levels of per capita income nor the structures of their economies truly qualifies them as anything other than countries at the upper end of the world's distribution of income. Indeed, it is only through the chicanery of using highly arbitrary exchange rates that Hungary and Romania can qualify as developing countries. The creation of the European Bank for Reconstruction and Development (BERD) is thus a particularly apt one, as the Bank will undertake long-term lending to East Europe, thus providing needed long-term capital for infrastructure and development in the region without compromising the integrity of World Bank rules or creating a direct competition between East Europe and the Third World for World Bank funds. Indeed, BERD is the prototypical organization designed expressly for the expansion of East-West relations, without impinging on the operation of existing western institutions, and thus serves as a conceptual model for the other institutions proposed here.

Although a portion of the BERD's lending will be directed toward private or cooperative enterprises in East Europe, most lending will go toward new businesses. Consequently, there will continue to be a lack of funds for the purchase of large state-owned enterprises by residents of those East European countries where privatization of industry will be allowed. This will create a variety of problems. Lack of funds will slow the pace of privatization, leaving too many assets in state hands. At the same time, the privatization that does take place will occur either through sales to domestic financial institutions or to foreigners. In neither case are broad-based property ownership interests created among the population; moreover, in the case of foreign purchases, antagonism against foreign owners, especially those who make what are perceived as excessive profits or who fire redundant workers, will flare up, and, indeed, already has flared up in Hungary. Thus, political support for privatization and for marketizing reforms will be jeopardized.

Two measures are needed. The first is to develop some mutually agreed upon guidelines for western investment in the Soviet Union and East Europe. East European governments currently face intense pressure to liberalize foreign investment rules, yet none has the time or in some cases ability to think these issues through carefully. The negative experience of the developing countries with their first wave of foreign direct investment need not, and ought not, be repeated in East Europe. Nor should the focus of such a scenario keep the East European countries from obtaining the benefits that foreign direct investment from the West could bring. Thus, an exchange of experience and mutual restraint and cooperation would do much to maintain harmony in a politically sensitive area of expanding East-West cooperation.

In addition to BERD lending to new private enterprises, funds should be provided to assist local entrepreneurs to acquire state-owned enterprises and for the population at large to participate in stock ownership. Funds to facilitate such privatization ought to be raised in both the East and the West through a cooperative effort. Western governments could tax, at very low rates, their firms' investments in, or profit remittances from, the East, thus generating hard currency funds. Participating East European countries would agree to earmark a portion of their taxes on foreign-owned firms to the creation of counterpart funds in the domestic currency. A special bank for this purpose, or a special facility of the BERD, would be established with branches in the West, where additional funds could be raised on credit markets, and in each participating East European country, where loans would be made, to manage these funds.

Thus, the bank would, for example, provide long-term credits to entrepreneurs or workers in an eastern country that wished to purchase and operate a state-owned enterprise or to bid for a foreign-owned firm. Loans could also be made to finance new firms. In either case, the bank could lend in either domestic currency or in foreign currency as appropriate. Because East European entrepreneurs are unlikely to have access to foreign capital markets, while domestic capital markets will be underdeveloped, such a

bank would be the only means by which the residents of East
Europe could be placed on an equal footing with foreigners in the
competition for the ownership of indigenous capital.

Trade Facilitation

An important measure to facilitate East-West trade is the standard-
ization of international trade and payments standards and conventions and statistical reporting and accounting standards.   In this
area, the reliance on western institutions can be greater.   For example, eastern countries should join and accede to the principles
and practices of the International Chamber of Commerce and similar standard-setting bodies.   In those cases where expertise lies in
western bodies such as the World Bank or the IMF, alternatives
such as the OECD or the United Nations Economic Commission for
Europe should be sought.

Graduation

The institutions proposed here should be viewed as temporary,
though the process of systemic change in East Europe is likely to be
longer than many suspect.   Thus, it should be expected that, as individual East European countries progress toward marketization
and destatization at their own pace, they will reach a point at
which membership in western organizations such as the GATT or
the Bretton Woods institutions or even the EC will be feasible instead of, or in addition to, membership in these special East-West
institutions.   Until all eastern countries are able to reach such a
stage of integration, these institutions will continue to serve a useful purpose.   The role of eastern countries within these organizations will of course change, as those countries whose reforms prove
more successful, or are implemented more rapidly, increasingly
assume roles more similar to those played by developed market
economies.   In this way, the integration of the eastern countries
into the world economy can occur at an evolutionary and sustainable pace.

CONCLUSIONS

The problems of integrating the reforming countries of East Europe into the world economy will be long-term and are unlikely to be solved by reliance on existing western institutions designed to mediate and promote international commerce. New and innovative institutions are needed and ought to be discussed at the Madrid meetings of the Conference on European Cooperation and Security, as well as at other East-West fora.

5

Economic Reform in the Soviet Union: The Process, the Changing Perception, and the Role of the Financial Sphere

Vladimir T. Musatov

This paper explores important changes that have taken place recently in the transformation of the Soviet economy and in the perception of this process. Such analysis is necessary in order to stress the utmost importance of what is happening and should happen in the financial sphere and to put the events in this sphere in the broad context of the radical economic reform.

The final goal of the reform is still defined, with some variations, as the creation of a socialist market economy, a planned-market economy, and a regulated market economy. But there is a growing shift, as the stress now is increasingly put on the word "market." The phrase "regulated market economy" is supported by a growing number of economists and politicians, and it has a good chance to become the dominant definition. In any case, it is now clear that the presence of full-fledged markets will be the main feature of the future Soviet economy. There is not only more clarity with the final goal, but also with the starting point, which is this question: What is being transformed into a market-type economy?

The simplest questions are often very difficult to answer. Especially when the answers seem to be obvious and are common knowledge. The answer to the question "What is the main difference between the western and socialist economic systems?" is usually given in an instinctive, automatic way. Indeed, in numerous textbooks and reference books the notion of a centrally planned economy as opposed to a market economy is of paramount importance.

41

If it is so, and the traditional answer is correct, then the transition we are now undergoing is a transition from a centrally planned economy to a market economy. There are economists who argue, however, that the transition is from a distorted market economy to a genuine market economy.

This might seem paradoxical, but our economy in reality probably was closer to the market-type economy than to the centrally planned economy. Let us take the position of the consumer. If he or she is given the right to choose what to buy, then the place where he uses this right should be called "market," that is, the natural meeting place for the producer and consumer. The only way to construct an economy without a market is to prevent the consumer from meeting the producer, that is, to designate certain consumers to receive goods made by certain producers. This means strict rationing. The essence of the process called "planning" becomes not planning as such, but the distribution of investment and consumer goods and resources needed to produce them. Such measures can help a devastated country to overcome the consequences of war and even make initial steps toward industrialization.

Initially, central distribution of resources results in an increase in the volume of production, which makes possible the lifting of strict rationing of consumer goods. People do not like, quite understandably, strict rationing. The rationing of investment goods remains, but the economic system loses its homogeneity. Central distribution will be scrapped sooner or later, and it becomes simply a question of time. Two elements of the economic system—the right of the consumer to choose and the obligation of the producer to make what he is told to make by a central authority—simply cannot coexist for long. If the consumer is free to choose, then the producer should be free to decide what to produce.

The consumer's right to choose is the crucial component of the market economy. After this component is introduced, market forces begin to act, and the transition from a distorted market to the market in the proper sense of the word begins. This transition began in the 1960s, not in 1985. There is much talk in our literature about several unsuccessful attempts to reform the economy. Characteristically, those who opposed the pre-perestroika reforms and eventually thwarted attempts to transform the economy did it on ideological grounds—they were against the market economy and firmly stood for the planned economy. The proponents of the reforms often believed that their main task was to increase the efficiency of planning. It seems that neither side understood correctly that it confronted the distorted market. The problems they had to deal with were caused not only by the administrative bureaucracy but also, and increasingly, by market forces.

Even after perestroika began, it took several years for the majority of the economists to understand that the only solution to our economic problems was the creation of a market economy. Now this goal is proclaimed. But still only rarely voices can be heard stating that we already and for several decades had a peculiar kind of a market economy, one with a market that became more and more distorted. The failure of previous reforms aggravated the situation. It can be assumed that the transition from a planned economy (that is, the economy where everything is rationed) to a market economy is easier than the transition from a distorted market to a normal market. It seems that the realities of our economic life corroborate such an assumption.

Under the system of strict rationing (including jobs) there should be no unemployment and no money overhang. Of course, in the longer run strict rationing cannot keep the economy in good shape; disproportions inevitably appear and become more evident, as does the inherent inability of an economy where everything is rationed to innovate. At least, however, the rationed economy is essentially a balanced economy—the distortions, after they develop, remain relatively minor.

Market forces, after they are introduced through the behavior of consumers, gradually undermine the rationing in the capital-goods sector by aggravating the distortions. Medicine is often made from poison. Side effects of a medicine are sometimes more difficult to cure than the illness itself. I mention this to stress the following three points:

1. During the last year a dramatic change in the mentality of many Soviet economists and leading public figures occurred: They realized that the real goal of perestroika in the economic sphere was the building of a regulated market economy. The illusions about the possibility of modifying the existing system of planning were gone. At the same time, it became clear that

a package of drastic measures is needed to place the producers into the market environment.

2. After the awareness of the necessity to build a market economy became firmly rooted, the next logical conclusion was drawn: the country needs all the basic elements of the market, including such elements that not long ago seemed completely unacceptable in a socialist society. As a result, a lot of rethinking about the future of our financial system was done. The introduction of securities markets, stock exchanges, and private shareholding began to be discussed as something practical, something that was no longer ideologically taboo. Many economists and politicians realized that the existence of private farms and securities markets could be reconciled with the maintenance of social equality, with the prevention of social deprivation. All this might seem quite obvious, but it was a giant step forward.

3. Now it becomes increasingly clear that reforms in the financial sphere cannot be put aside for a while and postponed until the end of the transition period. If we are moving toward a market economy, then financial reforms are very traumatic for the population and for the economy. Nevertheless, decisive steps are needed, even if they are on the verge of shock therapy.

It can be argued, of course, that it is not for the first time that financial problems came to the forefront of the radical economic reform. Several years ago the introduction of new prices was actively discussed. There is a great difference, however, between today's situation and those discussions, because now the whole range of problems connected with money, banking, and prices is perceived in a systemic way. The interdependence among new prices, the convertible ruble, securities markets, a central bank, and commercial banking was realized.

I take great pains to stress that many, but not all, economists came to the conclusions formulated above. It is natural for economists to quarrel, and nobody would be surprised to hear, for example, that a meeting at which three economists took part produced five different options. The problem is not with economists but with the population, a large part of which is still afraid of the market economy. This part still thinks that we had a planned economy, and that the state is responsible and should remain responsible for the day-to-day running of the economy, for the availability of goods. I am still of the opinion, which was reinforced by recent events, that changes in the mass psychology are crucial for the success of the economic reform. It is extremely important for our people to realize that they already live partly under market conditions, that the market—albeit distorted—began when they as consumers received the possibility to choose what to buy. And if they want to retain this right, they must support the transition to the market economy and share part of the burden associated with such transition.

Unfortunately, new forms of economic activity—cooperatives, for example—evoke anger or even wrath in many people. But the problem is that the defects of the old system appear to be the defects of the nascent market mechanisms. The old system is responsible for the creation of conditions under which state enterprises and consumers were put at a disadvantage while cooperants enjoyed the privilege of receiving fabulous—and undeserved—profits, which offended public morality.

In general, the perception of cause-and-effect links is often inadequate, and it slows down the speed of changes in the economy and reinforces old cliches in the mass psychology. The perception of the role the underground economy plays during transition to a market economy is one of the striking examples. Black marketeers are rumored to be very interested in such transition. Underground entrepreneurs, the story goes, will use their wealth to acquire means of production. In reality, the transition to a normal market simply will mean the end of the underground tycoons, who will not survive the transition. The main source of profits for them was not the business that was illegal in a normal market economy (for example, drugs and gambling), but the distortions caused by the overcentralized distribution system and shortages of goods and services. It would be only natural for such black marketeers to oppose changes, to instigate protests. The public, however, thinks otherwise.

What are the main impediments on the road to a genuine market economy? Before giving a list of them, it should be stressed that the relative importance of each obstacle changes due to the systemic changes in the sociopolitical and economic situation.

Such changes might be abrupt or gradual, sensational or almost unnoticed. One way or another, they shed new light at the evolution of the nascent market. Furthermore, the removal of one obstacle might dramatically enhance the importance of another obstacle, so there is no certainty that all problems to be solved during the transition phase to the market economy are well known or properly understood.

For example, there was a broad consensus that the enterprises should be given freedom in their activities, that they should be made less dependent on branch ministries. It is inconceivable to build a market without giving the enterprises the right to decide what they will produce and in what amounts. Enterprises today enjoy a much greater independence from central economic bodies than before 1985. Many of our enterprises always were monopoly producers, and now they became, in a sense, independent monopoly producers. Under the old system, the branch ministries—the holders of a 100 percent monopoly and responsible for the decisionmaking process of the enterprises—somehow tamed the aspirations of each other to use the monopoly position to the disadvantage of their counterparts. The oft-criticized central bodies responsible for the distribution of material resources or the functioning of the price-setting mechanism also contributed to the neutralization of monopolistic effects. The old economic order was a system that had all the necessary elements allowing it to function.

The enterprises used their newly found (though by no means complete) freedom as an experienced monopolist would: by beginning to diminish the volume of production and to raise prices. The first way was easier to take because prices remained largely regulated. The enterprises in many cases had a serious reason to argue that they were forced to decrease the production, as they have no other possibility to get rid of obsolete equipment. Previously, the ministries often prevented them from doing it because the well-being of the ministries depended on their ability to report the steady growth of production, which is why the 100 percent use of industrial capacity became one of the main features of the Soviet economy and one of the main causes of its inefficiency.

So, the first main obstacle that has to be overcome is the monopoly position of many producers. The newly born market cannot be left at the mercy of monopolists. This situation is one more example of the problem mentioned above: Ordinary people think that the decrease in the supply of goods and rising prices are caused by the market—that is, by the market that was the final goal of the reform—and not by the legacy of the former system. The reform of the pricing system can only aggravate the problem, because enterprises will be given more freedom in setting the prices.

The second main obstacle is the lack of motivation for working people. The government is extremely worried that wages and salaries are growing much faster than labor productivity. Many items that could be bought freely disappeared. Economists are talking about the consumer market falling apart. Under such circumstances, the government tries to limit the growth of money incomes. At the same time, inflation accelerates, primarily due to the budget deficit. Thus, where is the reason to work harder? Prices for basic necessities are stable, and other goods are either impossible to buy at whatever price or can be bought at such prices that are unaffordable due to the restrictions on incomes.

It is often stated in our press that the main problem is the widening gap between the money supply and the volume of material resources reaching the market (and taking the form of investment or consumer goods). It can be argued that the present-day economic policy is very much deflationary in character, that it is primarily aimed at limiting the growth of money supply. In my opinion, the main emphasis should be placed firmly at measures stimulating the output of goods and services. The imbalance between the money supply and available goods and services should be dealt with not only from the monetary end, but also and primarily from the opposite end, that is, by increasing the availability of goods. Deflation is probably now more dangerous than inflation. The infamous monetary overhang constitutes, clearly enough, a very serious problem. But it would be wrong to assume that the liquidation of the monetary overhang would be tantamount to the successful financial reform. A much broader spectrum of measures is needed to set the financial house in order. Furthermore, such measures can be successful in the longer run only if monopoly aspirations of the producers are checked and there are extensive possibilities to stimulate the workers.

In a sense, deflationary measures could block financial reforms. The main purpose of the financial reforms should be viewed as the creation of an economic environment conducive to stable economic growth, to active innovation on the part of producers. Financial reforms should correspond to other important measures, primarily to tax reform. The desire to raise taxes to balance the budget could thwart all other attempts to create a normal market economy. The main ways to balance the budget should be the cutting of irrational expenses and the growth of economic activity so that revenues increase.

It became sufficiently clear that financial reforms would be ineffective without the transformation of the banking system. We can discern two stages in the banking reform. The first led to the creation of the so-called specialized banks and was restricted to the splitting of Gosbank into several banks specialized along branch lines, without major changes in the principles of banking that were typical in past decades. The second stage, as opposed to the first, was not initiated from above—it began spontaneously and took the form of creation of commercial banks by enterprises and cooperatives. Now a third and final stage is badly needed. It should lead to the creation of a full-fledged central bank as its highest tier and a system of regulated commercial banks as its second tier. All banks belonging to the second tier should be put on equal footing, and the remnants of monopoly positions enjoyed until now by the specialized banks that appeared at the first stage of the reform should be scrapped. The third phase of the banking reform should create banks in the proper sense of the word. Under the administrative economic system, banks merely distributed financial resources allocated to the enterprises or large individual projects by the central authorities. If this is taken into account, it is possible to explain the symbolic rate charged for long-term loans.

Another point worth mentioning is the need to enact all the important reforms more or less simultaneously. Only the realization of this precondition will create favorable circumstances in which new financial mechanisms will work.

The main implications of the new understanding of the final goal of economic restructuring for the financial sphere can be summarized in this way: After completion of the transition period, the Soviet economy will have a wide range of financial markets common for a regulated market economy. New credit and financial institutions will appear that will provide new financial services, and the scheme of financial flows will be different from what we have now.

The question of the speed with which we will be moving toward a market economy is of paramount importance. I tried to stress the point that our country was "pregnant," so to speak, with a market economy for a long time. But it is impossible to be pregnant indefinitely. The time has come for decisive endeavor.

6

What Congress and the Administration Can Do to Improve Soviet–U.S. Trade Relations

Peter J. Pettibone

Our nation's trade policy with the Soviet Union is more complex than the trade policies of many of our allies, where the principal, and in some cases the only, interest is a commercial one. Because our trade policy has often sought to restrict trade with the Soviet Union in order to accomplish other goals, our business leaders have been at a distinct disadvantage in their commercial transactions in the Soviet Union. For example, the Jackson-Vanik Amendment to the Trade Act of 1974[1] conditions most favored nation (MFN) status to the Soviet Union and certain other communist countries on freedom of emigration. Another example was the imposition in 1981 and 1982 of restrictions on the supply of equipment for the construction of the Urengoi natural gas pipeline to protest the Soviet role in the imposition of martial law in Poland.

The rapid political changes that have occurred in East Europe and the Soviet Union during the past few months, the improvements in emigration and other human rights in the Soviet Union, and the continuing democratization of the Soviet government through national and local elections have created a new business environment and many new opportunities for trade and investment in the Soviet Union. Business leaders in other western countries and in the Far East are moving rapidly to take advantage of these opportunities. However, U.S. business leaders are falling behind in taking advantage of these opportunities, in part because

---

1. Section 402 of the Trade Act of 1974, 19 U.S.C. § 2432.

51

of existing trade constraints. This paper will describe certain actions that Congress and the Bush administration can take to improve trade relations between the United States and the Soviet Union.

ADOPT A NEW TRADE AGREEMENT

In 1972, during the period of détente, the United States and the Soviet Union signed a trade agreement granting reciprocal MFN status to the products of the two countries. The 1972 trade agreement was never implemented because the Jackson-Vanik Amendment barred the grant of most favored nation status to nonmarket economy countries that did not permit freedom of emigration. Although levels of emigration from the Soviet Union had been relatively high in the late 1970s, the Soviet Union was unwilling to give the U.S. government assurances that those levels of emigration would continue, and the 1972 trade agreement was never implemented.

Nearly all the commentators on the subject of Soviet-U.S. trade have advocated that a new trade agreement should be entered into in order to improve the prospects for U.S. businesses in the Soviet Union. President Bush, at the Malta Summit meeting in December 1989, set as a goal the conclusion of a trade agreement by the time of the June 1990 Summit in Moscow. The first round of negotiations on a new trade agreement was held in Washington in February. A second round of negotiations was held in London in early March, and a third round is scheduled for Vienna in late March.[2]

Certain commentators believe that the starting point for a new trade agreement should not be the 1972 trade agreement or other trade agreements that have been negotiated with nonmarket economies, such as the trade agreement between the U.S. and China. Rather, they have suggested that a new trade agreement with the Soviet Union should cover not only such standard provi-

2. On June 1, 1990, the presidents of the United States and the Soviet Union signed a Trade Agreement that incorporates many of the suggestions discussed in the section of the chapter.

sions as trade promotion and commercial arrangements,[3] but should address the practical problems of doing business between the two countries.

For example, a new trade agreement should address the lack of available hard currency in the Soviet Union It might, for example, seek a commitment from the Soviets to allocate a certain percentage of foreign exchange for the direct purchase of U.S. products. Or, a U.S. company might be given hard currency credits by the Soviet government for new products produced in the Soviet Union for the internal market that displace products currently being imported into the Soviet Union (import substitution). A new trade agreement might also address the difficulties U.S. businesses encounter in establishing Soviet offices by improving the accreditation process and securing commitments from the Soviet government to assist in making office space and housing available for U.S. business representatives, by improving telecommunications facilities, and by permitting foreign companies to establish ruble bank accounts as well as foreign exchange bank accounts in the Soviet Union.

A new trade agreement might further require the Soviet government to develop an adequate economic statistical base, which would facilitate decisionmaking by U.S. businesses.

Finally, a new trade agreement might remove restrictions on U.S. companies hiring Soviet staff, by allowing them to hire from the general population and to dismiss unsatisfactory employees.

As noted above, the reason that the 1972 trade agreement was never implemented was the enactment of the Jackson-Vanik Amendment in 1974. President Bush has said that, if the Soviets enact an emigration law, he will seek a one-year waiver of the Jackson-Vanik provisions barring the grant of MFN status to Soviet products. Such a one-year waiver is contemplated by the existing provisions of the Jackson-Vanik Amendment and would not require congressional action to amend or repeal Jackson-Vanik. The

3. Section 405 of the Trade Act of 1974 (19 U.S.C. § 2435) mandates certain provisions that must be included in a trade agreement with a country previously denied MFN status. These include: (1) the initial term of the agreement can be for no more than three years; (2) the agreement must be subject to suspension or termination on national security grounds; (3) it must contain safeguards against market disruption; (4) it must provide arrangements for the protection of industrial rights and processes; (5) it must provide for the settlement of commercial differences and disputes; and (6) it must contain certain trade promotion provisions.

Soviet negotiators on a new trade agreement are pressing for a three-year waiver of Jackson-Vanik, which would require congressional action, and most U.S. commentators have argued for either a multiyear waiver or outright repeal of Jackson-Vanik.

The principal reasons given for a long-term waiver or repeal are that this action would encourage joint venture investments by U.S. businesses in the Soviet Union, which are longer term in nature and would benefit greatly if MFN status could be guaranteed to be available for more than just a one-year period. A long-term waiver or repeal would particularly help small and medium-sized American companies, which need to access the American market in order to sell products of their joint ventures. Many small and medium-sized U.S. companies that seek to enter into joint ventures in the Soviet Union do not have extensive distribution arrangements in other parts of the world, and the natural market for the products of their joint ventures is the United States. The lack of MFN treatment accorded the products of their joint ventures puts these small and medium-sized American companies at a competitive disadvantage. For example, if a U.S. company and a German company are competing for the same export-oriented joint venture opportunity in the Soviet Union, the German company would have a distinct advantage in the negotiations because the products of the joint venture would be accorded MFN treatment in Germany.

Also, because the tariff structure in the Soviet Union is based on the principle of reciprocity, the lack of MFN status may mean that higher duties will be imposed on imports of U.S. goods into the Soviet Union, making them less competitive than imports from West Europe.

While I personally have advocated a long-term waiver or repeal of Jackson-Vanik, I expect that the agreement submitted to Presidents Bush and Gorbachev at the June Summit will be based upon a one-year waiver.

REPEAL LEGISLATION THAT PREVENTS THE EXTENSION OF EXPORT CREDITS AND LOAN GUARANTEES

There are three legislative acts restricting export credits and loan guarantees in U.S.-Soviet trade that should be repealed in order to improve the competitive position of U.S. companies in the Soviet market. The first is the Stevenson Amendment,[4] which prohibits the Export-Import Bank and any other agency of the U.S. government (other than the Commodity Credit Corporation) from approving loans, guarantees, insurance, or any combination of these, for exports to the Soviet Union in amounts in excess of US$300 million without prior congressional approval as provided by law. Because this amount has already been reached for all practical purposes, the effect of the Stevenson Amendment is to bar any further credits, guarantees, or insurance for exports to the Soviet Union by the Export-Import Bank and any other U.S. governmental agency (other than the Commodity Credit Corporation). In contrast, major western governments have outstanding commitments, totaling approximately US$16 billion, to support exports to the Soviet Union. More than two-thirds of this amount has been committed by four countries: Japan, Germany, France, and Italy. The consequence of the ready availability of export financing from these countries places the U.S. business representative who needs financing for export sales into the Soviet Union at a distinct disadvantage.

The second legislative act that should be repealed is the Byrd Amendment,[5] which prohibits loans or guarantees by the Export-Import Bank in amounts in excess of US$40 million in connection with research or exploration relating to fossil fuel energy resources in the Soviet Union.

The third legislative act that should be repealed is Section 620(f) of the Foreign Assistance Act of 1961,[6] which restricts the Overseas Private Investment Corporation (OPIC) from offering insurance or guarantees for projects in any communist country. Recent legislation enables OPIC to provide investment guarantees for U.S. investments in Hungary and Poland,[7] but the restrictions of the 1961 act are still in force for U.S. investments in the Soviet Union.

A fourth piece of legislation that should be reconsidered in light of the recent moves in the Soviet Union and East Europe in

4. Section 613 of the Trade Act of 1974, 19 U.S.C. § 2487.
5. The Byrd Amendment to the 1974 Amendments to the Export-Import Bank Act, 12 U.S.C. § 635e(b).
6. 22 U.S.C. § 2370(f).
7. Foreign Operations, Export Financing, and Related Programs Appropriations Act, 1990, Pub.L. No. 101-167, § 597, 103 Stat. 1195, 1257 (1989).

the direction of market economies is Section 406 of the Trade Act of 1974,[8] which provides for safeguards against market disruptions caused by surges of imports from nonmarket economies. This provision and the provisions of the U.S. antidumping laws related to nonmarket economy imports have consistently proven to be cumbersome and unpredictable, and they need to be revised to take into account the changing nature of East Europe and the Soviet Union. At the same time, these laws need to recognize the very legitimate interest of U.S. businesses in being protected from injury caused by unfair commercial practices by East European and Soviet businesses.

SUPPORT THE SOVIET UNION'S REQUEST
TO BE GRANTED OBSERVER STATUS IN THE GATT

President Bush, at the Malta Summit, stated that the administration would support the Soviet Union's request to be granted observer status in the General Agreement on Tariffs and Trade (GATT) after the conclusion of the Uruguay Round. Observer status would help the Soviet Union move to a market system by involving it in western customs, tax, antitrust, and foreign exchange practices.

Some commentators have recommended that the administration, in consultation with its western allies and OECD trading partners, should devise economic reform "benchmarks" to monitor Soviet progress toward a market-driven economy. They have argued that these "benchmarks" would provide support to those working for economic reform within the Soviet Union while also protecting the GATT from the negative effects of integrating a huge, centrally planned economy into the world trading system.

IN COORDINATION WITH THE OTHER COCOM MEMBERS,
REVISE OUR APPROACH TO EXPORT CONTROLS

The Export Administration Act (EAA) will expire on September 30, 1990. While there has been some discussion about a major overhaul of the EAA, the Bush administration has indicated that it

---

8. 19 U.S.C. § 2436.

will seek a simple one-year extension.   Even leading members of Congress, such as Representative Gejdenson, Chairman of the Trade Subcommittee of the House Foreign Affairs Committee, have ruled out a massive revision to the EAA, suggesting that only the following problems might be addressed in legislation:

1. further streamlining and clarification of the procedure for determining and implementing assessments of foreign availability for a controlled product;
2. expansion of judicial review of the implementation of the EAA by the Executive Branch;
3. clarification of the overlapping jurisdiction of the departments of State and Commerce over "dual-use" items (having both commercial and military applications); and
4. publication of the administration's COCOM agreements.

Currently, the U.S. position (reflecting the views of the Defense Department) on COCOM controls is that it would like COCOM to adopt the so-called PRC Green Line controls for Czechoslovakia, Poland, and Hungary but maintain stricter controls for the Soviet Union. Certain major West European members of COCOM apparently believe that the more liberal standards of the PRC Green Line should be applicable not only to East Europe but also to the Soviet Union. Presently, it does not appear that the United States will adopt this more liberal position, thus placing U.S. businesses at a competitive disadvantage to the extent that other COCOM members allow companies in their countries greater freedom from export controls.

What is needed, both domestically and in the context of COCOM, are export controls that are limited to those goods and technologies that are truly strategic and consistent with the controls applied by the rest of COCOM.

ADOPT MORE REALISTIC VISA RESTRICTIONS FOR SOVIET BUSINESS LEADERS

The United States currently is significantly restricting the number of Soviet business representatives who come here either for training or to conduct business. These restrictions are a vestige of the Cold War and appear to be imposed because of intelligence concerns. For example, the B-1 visa, which is the normal business visa, was recently limited to a duration of 45 days for Soviet visitors. Therefore, American companies wishing to bring Soviets to the United States for training programs now must go through the lengthy process of obtaining an H-3 trainee visa.

The other type of visa available for Soviet business leaders is the L-1 intracompany transfer visa. For reasons of reciprocity, there is a very low quota on the number of L-1 visas that may be granted at any one time. This has resulted in a situation in which many U.S. companies have been unable to bring Soviet business leaders to this country. With the conclusion of more joint ventures and the resulting intracompany transfer requirements, this situation will become even more exacerbated unless the quotas are removed or significantly raised.

Congress and the administration should remove these artificial limits so that visa applications by Soviet business representatives can be decided on a case-by-case basis by the Immigration and Naturalization Service and the departments of State, Commerce and Justice.

NEGOTIATE A BILATERAL
INVESTMENT PROTECTION TREATY

The Soviet Union has already entered into bilateral investment protection treaties with Finland, Belgium, Germany, Great Britain, and Canada. These treaties create a favorable legal and psychological environment that enhances investments by investors in one country in the other. Providing legal protection for investments in the form of a treaty gives added assurance over protections that can be provided by local legislation because treaties cannot be unilaterally repudiated except on well-defined grounds.

A bilateral investment protection treaty between the United States and the Soviet Union would define: (1) what is a protected investment; (2) who is a protected investor; and (3) the level of protection. Some of the investment protection treaties that the Soviet Union has entered into with other western countries provide a "most favored nation status" to investments by investors in the other country. That is, the protection accorded to investors in the treaty country is no less favorable than the protection accorded investors in any other third country. Another form of protection is "national treatment," that is, the same rules and regulations that govern domestic investments and investors would be applicable to investments by investors from the other country. Some treaties select the higher of the two standards, and this is likely to be the standard in a U.S.-Soviet treaty. Often, these treaties will carve out exceptions for specified existing or future arrangements, such as present or future customs unions or mutual economic assistance pacts.

A bilateral investment protection treaty should also deal with the subject of expropriation. It would provide that expropriation is not permitted unless it is for a public purpose and only then if it is accompanied by prompt, adequate, and effective compensation. In the case of a U.S.-Soviet treaty, compensation by the Soviet Union payable to a U.S. investor by reason of the treaty would have to be paid in convertible currencies. The treaty would also provide for judicial review of the taking and a judicial determination of the value of that which was taken.

A bilateral investment protection treaty should also cover the subject of repatriation of capital and profits. The Soviet-German investment protection treaty contains a provision that appears to provide that German investors may repatriate profits and capital in convertible currencies.[9] I understand that there is disagreement among Soviet authorities as to whether this provision is to be taken literally (that is, ruble profits may be repatriated in convertible currencies) or whether it merely means that repatriation may be made in convertible currencies only when and if such currencies are available.

Finally, these treaties typically provide for dispute resolution by international arbitration, thus providing a neutral forum for the protection of investors in the two contracting states.

9. Article 5 of the Treaty between the Federal Republic of Germany and the Union of Soviet Socialist Republics concerning Promotion and Joint Guaranty of Capital Investments (unofficial English translation).

NEGOTIATE AMENDMENTS TO THE
1973 U.S.-SOVIET INCOME TAX TREATY

Another factor resulting in American joint venture investments
being made through third countries is the lack of favorable Soviet
tax treatment accorded to dividends paid to American companies.
The 1973 U.S.-Soviet Income Tax Treaty is silent on the subject of
dividends, with the result that dividends payable to American
companies are subject to a 20 percent Soviet withholding tax.
Several countries, such as Cyprus and Austria, have income tax
treaties with the Soviet Union that exempt dividends paid to companies in those countries from the 20 percent Soviet withholding
tax. A protocol to add this exemption to the U.S.-Soviet Income Tax
Treaty was initialed in 1979 but shelved when the Soviets invaded
Afghanistan. It is now time to amend the U.S.-Soviet Income Tax
Treaty to provide this exemption.[10] The result will be that
American companies establishing joint ventures in the Soviet
Union no longer will need to consider forming subsidiaries in
countries such as Cyprus in order to achieve favorable tax treatment
for dividends.

Some commentators engaged in the construction industry have
also requested that the U.S.-Soviet Income Tax Treaty be amended to
include a clear definition of what constitutes a taxable presence or
permanent establishment in the Soviet Union.[11] These commentators have said that the tax treaty should specify that construction
projects, as well as building sites and installation and assembly
projects, do not constitute permanent establishments unless they
last more than 36 months, with the possibility of a longer period
in specific cases. (Such a provision appears in the current Finland-
USSR tax treaty.) These commentators also urge that a provision be
included to the effect that business profits may only be taxed if they
are directly attributable to a permanent establishment. Finally,
they recommend that it should be made clear in the treaty that income from services, including engineering services, is considered

10. On September 15, 1990, negotiators for the United States and the Soviet Union
initialed a new tax treaty between the two countries.
11. For example, Charles B. Hugel, Chairman of ASEA Brown Boveri, Inc.
(formerly Combustion Engineering Inc.), in testimony before the House Ways and
Means Committee, January 31, 1990.

business profits for this purpose, and, that if taxed in the Soviet Union, such income would constitute foreign source income for purposes of the U.S. foreign tax credit.

In conclusion, there are a number of actions that Congress and the administration can take at the present time that would enhance greatly the ability of U.S. businesses to compete in the Soviet market.

7

Soviet Financial Reform: Money and Credit

Francis A. Scotland

There is no worthy alternative to the market as a method of coordinating the activities and interests of economic agents.

—Document put forward by Deputy Prime Minister Leonid Albalkin at the All-Union Conference and Workshop on Problems of Radical Economic Reform, November 1989.

The Soviet leadership seems to be moving closer to embracing a market organized economy as its ideal and moving away from the confused notion of a system halfway between the economic extremes of central planning and market coordinated activity. This is a tremendous step forward. Self-serving reform and development of the financial system are impossible without embracing the tenets of a market-based system: namely, competition and freely determined prices. Correspondingly, the quicker the leadership embraces market-oriented structures and solutions, the sooner the economy will move away from the slow-motion contraction currently under way.

How can the Soviets attain their goal of financial market reform? The underlying assumption is that modern capital markets are the most efficient form of transferring financial resources from savers to creditworthy borrowers, and, in the process, optimal economic prosperity is achieved. The Soviet Union will prosper in the long run if it develops in a direction consistent with and directed toward financial market development.

My proposals are limited by a lack of precise detail about how the Soviet economy operates. In addition, it is difficult to conceive of how financial market reform can occur independent of corresponding economic reforms. Development of a stock market seems totally premature before resolving the issues of property rights, free-market price setting, and competition. As a result, many of the following financial reform proposals have elements of economic reform not fully elaborated.

The development of the Soviet economy on a centrally planned basis and the use of money as an administrative tool rather than as a means to effect economic allocation have short-circuited the problem of managing money. This has removed the potentially destabilizing impact of money that market-based economies have experienced occasionally. However, the cost of this stability has been great to Soviet society and to the country's economic progress. Going forward, financial reform can help rejuvenate growth and achieve a higher standard of living for all.

Numerous steps already have been taken in the Soviet Union toward the goal of a market-based system. The entrepreneurial zeal and spirit of competition are most apparent in banking, which is the cornerstone of financial systems in market economies. Private banks are springing up and, for a profit, are engaged in the business of arbitraging the liquidity preference of savers with the liquidity needs of borrowers. Changes are occurring so rapidly that some of the suggestions in this paper may be out of date.

But financial reform without the proper checks and balances along with economic reform is counterproductive and destabilizing. There already is some indication that the new banks are taking full advantage of their newly acquired freedoms, but the main macroeconomic signals they are reacting to are incorrect. Consequently, the new banks are efficiently engineering an even more rapid inflation and swelling overhang of unwanted rubles. A few insights into the Soviet Union's previous monetary and credit system is useful to understanding the situation.

THE OLD FINANCIAL SYSTEM: A WESTERN VIEW

A financial system per se did not exist under the previous system of planning beyond primitive but efficient savings banks. The role of "money" was as a unit of account and not a common store of value.

Money served two distinct groups. Workers or consumers were paid mostly in cash, which they used to buy goods and services. Enterprises also relied on money as a means of acquiring factors of production required to meet their production quotas. Once an enterprise acquired its certificate of allocation for needed materials, it presented its certificate to the Gosbank, which in turn granted the enterprise a credit, always a deposit transfer and rarely cash. The credit was used to acquire the corresponding inputs to production. It is obvious that the real store of wealth in this process is the state planning authority's allocation certificate.

The inefficiency of state planners has been well documented in official statistics and in the acid test of everyday living. Moreover, the system's inadequacies have become glaring when destabilizing macro-policies such as large budget deficits are imposed on the economy. The growing hoard of rubles (700 billion and rising) in the country is partly an accounting byproduct of the two independent consumer and producer sectors of the economy. It also reflects the unrecorded inflation caused by a budget deficit that the state planners failed to offset by reducing the allocation of resources to other sectors of the economy. The result is large queues instead of price inflation and/or strains on capital markets as in a market-determined economy.

TOWARD MARKET-BASED FINANCIAL REFORM

The current planning process should be completely reversed in order to implement a bona fide market-based financial system. The allocation certificates must become the unit of account and be relegated to an ex-post input/output description of the economy. And money must become a unit of value and not the unit of account. A central planner could envisage a public auction of allocation certificates with the quota given to the highest bidder. However, this is still too complicated and bureaucratic, and it limits the production and growth possibilities of the country to the imagination of the state planner.

Although there may be no textbooks on how to transform a centrally planned economy to a market-based economy, there is a wealth of knowledge growing out of recent Latin American experience. Four recurring themes have applications for the potential reform of the Soviet system:

1. Macroeconomic instability must be completely halted through control of fiscal and monetary policies before financial-sector reform can be accomplished. The absence of a bona fide monetary system in the Soviet Union puts heavy emphasis here on fiscal policy.
2. Decentralize economic decisionmaking and control from the bureaucrats and into the hands of those individuals and enterprises with the best incentives and the most amount of information. Adoption of this principle would be a radical departure from the current philosophy of central planning.
3. Prices must be allowed to move freely and to reflect shortages in order to stimulate investments. Competition is vital to this role.
4. Successful financial market reform in Latin America also has occurred by opening the economy to foreign investment and international trade through the elimination of export subsidies, tariffs, and import controls.

These proposals raise the complex question of the political economy. It is often said that there is no social consensus for market-based reform. The Latin American experience suggests that there is nothing new about this. The problems have arisen because vested interests have a stake in preserving the distortions that are the source of a country's dilemma. However, Latin America has shown that these kinds of problems only delay the inevitability of change and reform until the economic circumstances become even more desperate.

In addition, the experience of the United States in the late 1970s provides some insight for Soviet consideration. A policy debate developed during the 1970s on the merits of gradualism versus "cold-shower" shocks in the context of lowering inflation. The facts speak for themselves. It took the worst recession since the Great Depression in the 1930s to alter people's behavior sufficiently to reduce inflation from a core level of 10-12 percent to current levels of around 4-5 percent, a change that seems modest in comparison with the change in attitudes that must occur in the Soviet Union. The bigger the change in required behavior, the bigger the required shock. Gradual adjustments do not seem to work very well.

REFORM PROPOSALS

Some specific proposals in the area of financial market reform:

The Soviet Government Should Suspend State Planning Allocation Certificates as a Means to Resource Allocation

The starting point for this process would be the privatization of state enterprises as joint-stock companies. The state should give a portion of the shares so created to the workers in proportion to their salaries. (This assumes that private property rights have been resolved as an issue, and that the required litigation has been undertaken).

In return for this ownership, state enterprises no longer would be able to access a guaranteed allocation certificate from the state. Instead, the collective or "firm" would be required to bid for its resources using rubles. In addition, there would be no guarantee that wages would be paid if the output of the firm could not be sold. If output remains unpurchased, then the collective tries to compensate by raising its prices on the output it manages to sell, cuts wages or owner compensation, lays off people who are not owners, or goes out of business. This process introduces several factors crucial to a market-based economy: profitability and accountability, freely determined prices, risk, and ownership. It also creates a primary market in equities from which public participation would not be far off.

The development of the Soviet economy on a centrally planned basis and the use of money as an administrative tool rather than as a means to effect economic allocation have short-circuited the problem of managing money. This has removed the potentially destabilizing impact of money that market-based economies have experienced occasionally. However, the cost of this stability has been great to Soviet society and to the country's economic progress.

Going forward, financial reform can help rejuvenate growth and achieve a higher standard of living for all.

State collectives that make a profit should be free to use the profit as they see fit. Planners may worry that an orgy in consumer spending would ensue. But the odds are that the workers/owners of the collectives will quickly discover that it pays and/or sustains them in the long run to reinvest a substantial proportion of their profits in the firm. They might even consider that a western business education might be the most profitable form of R&D expenditure. Instead, worker/owners will discover that it is to their advantage to pay a premium for the best possible manager with the right skills. They will also discover that in order to attract the most suitable manager, they may have to offer him a direct interest in the business and, at some point, perhaps even controlling interest. Other businesses will discover the harsh reality that in a market-based economy there is no way for their firm to survive.

The government should take advantage of the changes by providing incentives to encourage capital investment and to discourage consumption in order to foster a strong manufacturing sector. This is an excellent chance to introduce a broadly based consumption tax.

As part of this process, individuals and organizations should be granted the freedom to establish enterprises where none have existed or to open businesses in sectors where they will compete with established state enterprises.

The biggest drawback to rapid privatization is acknowledging that in a market-based economy a good part of existing Soviet industry would go bankrupt and unemployment would rise sharply. Poland's experience shows that a major deflation is the first-round effect of a shift from central planning. Social benefit programs, therefore, must be established in order to provide the safety net common in most advanced industrialized nations.

Development of Financial and Economic Reform Will Be Incomplete Without Inflation Control as a Top Priority

This will be especially important as the ruble shifts from being a unit of account to a unit of value and a legitimate medium of exchange. Unless the Soviet Union can balance its budget, inflation will not be controlled without the development of a modern credit market that offers good compensation against the risk of inflation.

Specific steps toward financial reform to meet the goal of inflation control include the following:

1. Deregulate prices and allow the market to set prices.
2. There must be complete convertibility between the monetary system and the economy. Deposits and cash are interchangeable. Enterprises can acquire goods from any source.
3. Legislation should be created to give the central bank independent control over the liabilities on its balance sheet. Issuing credits in exchange for allocation certificates should be suspended and transferred to other government agencies. The central bank should work toward creating the financial infrastructure required to help it determine a noninflationary expansion in liquidity. Such measures would include:
   a. *Suspend Direct Credit Allocations*
      • Reorganize the public sector so that state subsidies are issued through a different agency. Raise financing through emerging capital markets.
   b. *Interest Rate Deregulation*
      • Deregulate the interest rate on all deposits.
      • Deregulate the interest rate on all commercial bank loans. This would allow commercial banks to price loans and deposits on the basis of risk and market demand.
   c. *Development of Banking Deposits*
      • Introduce new deposit instruments: demand deposits that pay no interest and fixed deposits that earn market interest rates on terms ranging from one month to five years.
   d. *Development of an Inter-Bank/Money Market*
      • Create negotiable certificates of deposit.
      • Grant rights to the direct issuance of commercial paper.
      • Foster the management of commercial bank liquidity needs (owing to reserve requirements and capital provisions) through the inter-bank market as well as

the money market.
- Use moral suasion, as in the Federal Reserve system, or effective penalties to inhibit a bank's use of a discount window at a rate subsidized below market levels.

These reforms would give the central bank a market mechanism to influence interest rates and overall credit conditions. Permitting nonbank access to this market encourages competition.

e. *Development of a Credit Market*
- Create a short-term government demand note akin to a U.S. Treasury Bill. An auction initially would be open to banks and eventually to licensed primary dealers.
- Create new classes of government debt with extending maturities. Their creation should be limited until a good secondary market has been established in short-term paper. (Reorganization of the public sector and the central bank will be impossible before this has been completed because rubles are the only source of financing that the government has for its deficit until government debt becomes available.) A market-determined auction would ensure that interest rates reflect monetary conditions.

Opening Up of the Domestic Financial System to the International Financial System

The ultimate goal should be to move toward full convertibility of the ruble with foreign currencies that will allow the integration of the Soviet economy into the world economy. To reach this goal:

1. Eliminate the labyrinth of subsidies given to state enterprises engaged in foreign trade and move toward a single exchange rate.
2. License foreign exchange dealers initially within the banking system to create a market in rubles.

SOME WARNINGS

It would be naive to regard financial market reform as a panacea or a substitute for the tough political and economic decisions that lie ahead. Successful financial reform is built on creating confidence both among Soviet citizens and in the world that the Soviet economy and government are able to honor the claims represented by the currency. Financial reforms put in place a structure that can help optimize performance as gains are made. But financial reform without attention to macroeconomic instability and market-clearing processes only fosters uncertainty and financial pressure. Modern financial markets in an economy such as the Soviet Union's likely would reflect fears of hyperinflation, skyrocketing interest rates, a freefall in the currency, and rapid growth in money and credit. This is hardly the financial backdrop required for sustainable growth.

Current reforms have already inspired a wave of new banking institutions in the Soviet Union. However, there is little indication that commercial banks have much incentive to make their lending decisions on the basis of risk and return or to bid very aggressively for deposits. Credit risk is still not an operating principle either for investors or enterprises because bankruptcy is not a permissible condition in the centrally planned system. Interest rates remain regulated. It is not clear what discretion commercial banks have over the composition of their balance sheets.

A STARTING POINT

The establishment of economic zones within which economic organization is entirely market-driven would be a second-best solution to this proposal, one that could allay some of the political-economic difficulties of rapid privatization. The zones would entail a smaller sector of the economy, but the privatization process could be much more radical.

Ownership in these zones would be private; the government would implement a basic taxation system with minimal expenditures for things such as infrastructure development.

A new currency would be created to be used in the new economic zone as well as an independent central bank within the zone to regulate supply of the new ruble. The currency would be completely convertible within the zone. A free-market rate of the new ruble for old rubles, however, would develop. Enterprises would quickly begin to operate on the basis of the two rubles, which in time would pave the way for the whole economy to shift to the new system.

A bold feature permitted by the use of economic zones could involve backing the new currency with the nation's stock of gold. The stock of gold likely is big enough, and the initial size of the enterprise zones would be small enough that the country's gold reserves would not be drained. The new zones very likely could issue bonds if the new ruble is backed by gold. The zones would be completely open to foreign ventures, including banks.

The free-enterprise zones would remove the primary obstacle to joint ventures and foreign direct investment in the Soviet Union: the lack of convertibility and the inability to repatriate profits without being drawn into the barter business.

BIBLIOGRAPHY

Hewett, Ed A. "Perestroika-Plus: The Albalkin Reforms." *PlanEcon Report*, Vol. V, No. 48-49.

Congdon, T. G. 1985. *Economic Liberalism in the Cone of Latin America.* Trade Policy Research Centre.

Garvey, George. "Policies and Mechanics Relating To Money." Federal Reserve Bank of New York.

McKinnon, R. J. 1973. *Money and Capital in Economic Development.* Washington, D.C.: Brookings Institution.

Shmelev, N., and V. Popov. 1989. *The Turning Point: Revitalizing the Soviet Economy.* New York: Doubleday.

The Institute of International Finance. 1990. *Building Free Market Economies in Central And Eastern Europe: Challenges and Realities.* April.

World Bank. 1989. *World Development Report.* Washington, D.C.: World Bank.

8

Models of
Capital Market Development

John A. Bohn, Jr., and David H. Levey

INTRODUCTION

The central focus of this paper is the question of whether credit risk, that is, the risk of default or delayed payment by a borrower, will exist in the Soviet financial system as it is further transformed, and, if so, within what institutional structure and by what procedures the required credit analysis will be performed.

The fundamental precondition for the insertion of credit risk into the Soviet system is elimination of the soft budget constraint for enterprises. This in turn must be preceded—or at least accompanied—by corporatization (if not true privatization) and price reform, so that managers freed from the constraints of physical planning can respond to a rational system of signals concerning demand and cost. Presuming, for the sake of the present discussion, that radical price and enterprise reform moves forward, there is still a choice to be made as to how the potential losses so created are measured, evaluated, and ultimately absorbed within the total system. How is the Soviet financial system likely to evolve given initial conditions and the forces and resistances that may be encountered as reform proceeds?

In approaching the question of capital market development in the Soviet Union, analysts have sometimes neglected to specify the institutional structure they are positing as the final goal of development, as if only one paradigm of financial structure existed in the developed market economies. Even a cursory view across the range of world financial markets, however, reveals a diversity of models, extending from the universal banking systems of much of continental Europe to the U.S.-type systems centered on autonomous equity and bond markets, along with a number of intermediate and transitional cases.

Each of these systems has its own particular mechanisms of providing long-term finance for industrial investment by private business enterprises. At the universal-banking end of the spectrum, finance is primarily provided by large banks within an oligopolistic structure, disclosure of company information is limited, default on obligations is almost unheard of, and credit analysis barely exists outside of the lending institutions. At the other extreme (labeled here for convenience the "U.S.-type model"), institutional and retail investors rely on advisory services and ratings—along with extensive disclosure—to make their decisions, and the risk of bankruptcy and/or default on debt obligations is relatively high.

Any concrete discussion of the creation of capital markets in the context of Soviet economic reform, therefore, must be careful to specify which model it has in mind as the end point of the proposed transformation, and it must also be concerned to show that this structure is compatible with the basic dynamic processes characteristic of the overall reform process and with the most likely tendencies present within the existing system. If not, the discussion runs the risk of being too abstract or even utopian.

One way to approach this issue is to list the conditions for the emergence and efficient functioning of a U.S.-type long-term corporate bond market. This list can be used in two ways: (1) to evaluate the likelihood that such conditions will be met, given the preferences of and constraints acting upon the economic authorities, and (2) to specify the concrete actions that need to be taken to implement creation of such a system, if the authorities so desire.

CONDITIONS FOR BOND MARKET DEVELOPMENT

1. Market determination of interest rates; gradual elimination of financial repression;

2. legal framework for collection of debts and resolution of disputes; bankruptcy law;
3. uniform accounting and auditing standards; formation of firms to carry out auditing function;
4. disclosure of financial information; communication of results to investors;
5. separation of commercial banking from underwriting and provision of financial advice; formation of appropriate intermediating institutions; and
6. formation of institutions to pool investible funds, such as life and casualty insurance companies, pension funds, and investment funds.

FORCES FAVORING UNIVERSAL BANKING

It is clear simply from the listing of such conditions that virtually all of them are missing from the Soviet scene and would be very difficult to create given the vast change in culture and behavior they presuppose and imply. The transition to a universal banking arrangement would seem more likely, given the presence of an already highly oligopolistic banking system, a tradition of spreading risk and loss across the population of savers and investors, that is, "socializing risk," and the authorities' desire to cushion the employment impacts of radical reform.

Movement in this direction would also be compatible with the thrust of banking-sector reform. It is one of the ironies of financial development that measures taken to strengthen banks—such as greater independence, strengthened capital adequacy, and improved professionalism in loan analysis—are likely to prevent or at least drastically slow the process of bond market development, as the banks move to a dominant position in industrial finance.

As corporatization proceeds, banks may find themselves owners of significant pieces of the enterprises that are insolvent when assets and liabilities are revalued using realistic prices. The authorities, operating under severe political pressure, may be tempted to slow down the process of redeploying labor by incorporating unrealized losses into the average spread between bank lending and

deposit rates, thereby spreading the risk across most of the population. Bank loan-loss reserves could be sustained out of the resulting
elevated earnings in the framework of an oligopolistic market
structure.

Enterprises, from their side, will prefer to acquire long-term
funds as well as working capital from the banks they have custom-
arily dealt with and with whose personnel they are familiar.
Analogously, on the funds supply side, Soviet households, without a
tradition of risk-taking, with initially less-than-full confidence in
the sustainability of reform, and with little information on the
true worth of enterprises, will prefer to hold their financial assets
in monetary form, particularly if a system of deposit insurance is
introduced.

In summary, then, there are many reasons to believe that the
path of least resistance for Soviet financial reform lies in the direction of universal banking rather than toward U.S.-style capital
markets. Two further questions follow: First, is there, consequently, no room for capital markets (and for independent credit
analysis) in the newly emerging Soviet system? And second,
should Soviet economic reformers be satisfied with the universal-
banking-type structure that appears to be the most likely outcome of
the system's own inherent tendencies, or should they take the steps
necessary to initiate the long process of creating the conditions for
a corporate bond market?

IMPLEMENTING SECURITIES MARKET FORMATION

Considering the first of the above questions, two areas stand out
clearly in which capital markets can and will develop, even in the
presence of universal banks: public-sector finance and interenter-
prise short-term lending ("commercial paper").

Soviet financial reform will be necessarily linked to budget reform. Financing of the central state deficit will rely increasingly
on marketing of bonds to households and enterprises as the state
restricts monetary expansion and attempts to immobilize the monetary overhang. This will require new issuing procedures and
formation of a secondary market. Banks will, as in so many developing market economies, use state bonds to satisfy statutory liq-

uidity requirements or to meet prudential risk-asset/capital ratios. In addition, decentralization of public-sector revenue collection and expenditures to republics, provinces, and municipalities will create the basis for an active "muni" market.

Enterprises with surplus funds will find it convenient to place some with enterprises in a cash-short situation, as a way of earning a higher return than may be available on bank deposits. Over time, and with the assistance of the appropriate legal and regulatory framework, a commercial paper market could emerge.

The second question posed above—whether a bond market for long-term finance of enterprise investment should be established—takes us into an area of ongoing debate among financial economists and historians concerning the advantages and disadvantages of universal banking. What might be called the "orthodox" position favoring the development of equity and bond markets is ably put forward in World Bank (1989), and its theoretical underpinnings are summarized in Fry (1988). The World Bank team argues that

> Liberalization should not be limited to the reform of the banking system but should seek to develop a more broadly based system that will include money and capital markets and nonbank intermediaries. . . . Active securities markets increase the supply of equity capital and long-term credit, which are vital to industrial investment. Experience in countries such as Malaysia and the Philippines suggests that the liberalization of commercial banking will not add much by itself to the availability of long-term credit and equity capital.

Economists at the International Finance Corporation (IFC) have in recent years been strong advocates for capital market formation and critics of universal and conglomerate banking. David Gill of the IFC has argued in several publications (Fry 1988, 282) that

> Generally, countries with "universal banking," such as Germany and France, have weaker contractual savings institutions and equity markets than countries which separate to some extent banking activities from securities markets activities, as in the U.S. and Canada. Bank dominance can lead to smaller equity markets than otherwise might be the case.

Fry (283) points out that

> Oligopolistic banking systems need more rather than less
> competition from direct financial markets.   Unless entry
> conditions are eased at the same time, a move towards universal
> banking may well reduce competition within the financial sector
> by increasing concentration.

This is a very relevant point for the Soviet Union, because the barriers to entry into banking and the degree of concentration are
likely to remain very high for the foreseeable future.

But the critique of universal banking by no means goes unchal-
lenged. Many economists (including, in fact, at the World Bank
and the IMF in the early 1980s) argue that universal banking alle-
viates financial instability and fragility and, by allowing banks to
take equity positions in client companies, prevents emergence of
excessive debt/equity ratios.   Many economic historians have
pointed out that the countries characterized by universal banking
have been among the fastest growing and claim that universal
banks are the easiest way to channel long-term funds to industry,
with the dynamic advantage of faster growth more than offsetting
any static loss from lower efficiency in the allocation of investment. It is also argued that large banks can substitute for state-
owned development finance institutions in the financing of very
large projects or those with a long payback period.

This is not the occasion, nor is the empirical evidence decisive
enough, to resolve these broader issues. Let us simply assume that
Soviet economic reformers have decided to create a system of securities markets. What are the steps that must be taken initially and
the most effective sequence of their introduction?

It appears likely that the broader process of property law and enterprise reform will shortly give rise to the issuance of shares to
banks and/or households.   The eventual trading of such shares
will necessitate creation of a stock exchange as well as a network of
financial intermediaries to operate the secondary market. At this
point, the question of whether to introduce legislation analogous to
the U.S. Glass-Steagall Act comes to the fore. If such a separation is
not mandated, it can be assumed that commercial banks will take
on these functions, which (along with the industrial shares they

may be allocated in the initial distribution) will lead them down the path to universal banking. A network of brokerage firms independent of the banks could become the locus of the development of credit analysis skills and later provide the infrastructure for bond issuance. This is the key decision point likely to determine the future shape of the Soviet financial system.

Government initiative will be essential in the establishment of accounting firms and the setting of uniform standards. Also, financial disclosure on a regular basis will be needed for all firms accessing the equity markets. The newly formed brokerage firms can begin to offer households and enterprises access to mutual funds and other devices for diversifying risk.

We expect, therefore, that the basic institutions and habits necessary for securities markets will first appear in connection with equity issuance and trading. Debt obligations will, for the most part, be claims of the banking system. The first stages of a bond market (beyond the previously mentioned markets for public-sector obligations) might involve term bond issues by the banks themselves, as they attempt to increase the average length of their liabilities. Over time, however, a process of disintermediation of long-term debt finance for other enterprises can begin to take place with the extension of rating activity into the industrial sector (from a prior base in the bank and municipal arenas) and formation of bond funds, as investors who previously held only government or municipal paper develop the confidence and information to diversify into industrial and bank issues.

THE ROLE OF A RATING AGENCY
IN DISINTERMEDIATED MARKETS

If the above development takes place over a period of time, it will be necessary to foster, or at least allow, the emergence of an independent and credible source of credit risk evaluation, that is, a rating agency. To understand the role a rating agency may play in fostering the Soviet Union's capital markets, it is important to understand the function the rating system currently fulfills in more-developed capital markets around the world.

The Rating Agency's Product

In essence, a rating agency promotes efficiency and stability in the marketplace by offering independent opinions on the future default risk of debt securities and related fixed-income obligations. Depending on investor demand, opinions may be offered on virtually any financial instrument that involves a promise to pay—including, but not limited to, corporate bonds, preferred stock, commercial paper, bank deposits, senior policyholder obligations of insurance companies, and structured financings.

Credit opinions are communicated to the marketplace in the form of ratings. These provide a quick, convenient means of ranking the risk of a range of debt instruments. In most cases, ratings and credit opinions are also communicated electronically and in print by means of research reports summarizing the rationale behind the rating judgments. Again, depending on investor needs, these may include new issue reports, company reports, industry reports, rating lists, and press releases.

The product of a rating agency is thus independent credit ratings and research. The process of "producing" these opinions generally includes regular meetings with the rated company's senior management and the compilation of analytical databases on each issuer and its industry. Those analytical databases that are used in publications are created with publicly available financial information. A rating agency will also develop databases for internal use that include confidential financial information provided by issuer management, which could include financial projections, hidden reserves, and so forth.

Ultimately, the analytical stage of the rating process is a function of the thinking of individual analysts and an evaluation of their conclusions in a "rating committee." Depending on the nature of each rating problem, rating committees can vary widely in size and duration. Generally, they include four or more members, at least one of whom is a member of senior rating agency management. Each committee has a lead analyst who is responsible for presenting a position report in support of what he or she judges the rating should be, taking into consideration the issuer's credit strengths and weakness. Such reports usually take into account myriad qualitative factors, such as management quality, industry trends, regulatory behavior, indenture provisions, and so forth, which are not readily reducible to statistics. Analyst recommendations can also make use of extensive analysis of financial ratios. Ultimately, the quality and success of an agency's rating opinions depend on the judgment and experience of its analysts, the integrity of its analytical process, and its track record at predicting defaults.

Rating's Value to Investors

A rating agency's opinions must provide value principally to important institutional investors. (Individual investors make some use of the rating agencies, but most of the public debt outstanding in the United States and the Eurobond markets is owned by several thousand major institutions.) These would include central and commercial banks, merchant banks, insurance companies, public- and private-sector pension funds, and many of the corporations who are also major borrowers. In fact, without investor perception of value, a rating agency's economic viability cannot be assured. From the investor's point of view, the ratings' central value is to serve as an accurate predictor of the likelihood of default of a given fixed-income investment. Investors use ratings to assess how much added return (or "risk premium") they should demand when purchasing a given security to compensate for the risk that the security will not perform as promised.

If ratings accomplish that central role, they may also fulfill a variety of related functions, such as:

1. Investors may use ratings to create "buy lists." For example, an investor institution's credit guidelines may stipulate that it may not buy or hold securities rated below a certain rating level.
2. Sophisticated institutions use ratings for comparative purposes—to compare risk-adjusted yields on a range of potential purchases or to monitor portfolio holdings in comparison with all other securities available in the marketplace at a given time. To create value for investors, it is thus necessary that a rating agency do the following:
   a. supply ratings on a "critical mass" of the major debt in-

struments and issuers in the marketplace; and
   b. alert investors in a timely manner when changes in
      issuer credit quality occur.
3. Aside from their use in fixed-income portfolio management,
   ratings are often employed by banks and other institutions to
   support decisions on corporate lending, inter-bank loans, trade
   finance, swap agreements, and other counterparty risk decisions.

It should be noted that ratings are essentially predictions of the future and that in most periods actual defaults are relatively few. The
ultimate accuracy of these predictions can only be known after a
bond has performed (or not performed) as promised. The immediate value of an agency's rating product must, therefore, be communicated to investors in other ways:

1. by assuring that the agency's rating opinions are objective and
   free from conflicts of interest;
2. by the quality and integrity of the agency's analytical staff;
3. by making it clear to investors that confidential information
   provided by the issuers is incorporated into the rating judgment. (Of course, such confidential information is communicated via the rating only and not in written materials or discussions with investors; in that way, confidentiality between
   the rating agency and the issuer is preserved); and
4. by publicizing the agency's ratings and research broadly to the
   marketplace, and by meeting regularly with major investors
   and developing research services attuned to their needs.

From the above, it should be obvious that for investors to recognize
the value of ratings, the following conditions must be present:

1. Investors must perceive that they are at risk of default on securities they purchase.
2. Investors must develop a relatively sophisticated understanding
   of portfolio management and credit risk analysis.

Because of their value to the markets, ratings are generally made
public to the marketplace as a whole. Having created value, how-

ever, the rating agency may charge investors for specialized research services and publications.

Rating's Value to Issuers of Debt

In more-developed credit markets, the major issuers of private-sector debt would include depository institutions, finance companies, securities firms, and industrial corporations. Governmental entities below the national level, such as cities, states, and provinces, also make use of credit ratings. If the agency's ratings and research are perceived by the markets as providing real value to investors (therefore influencing their purchase decisions), then ratings also provide substantial value to issuers of debt, such as:

1. Broadly disseminated credit opinions can provide wider access to investor capital, thus furnishing lower-cost borrowing and added financial flexibility. For example, as noted above, some institutional investors may not purchase debt securities rated below a certain level. Unrated issuers of whatever credit strength thereby may have a narrower investor base ready to purchase their debt.
2. In some cases, investors who otherwise would have required a bank guarantee to purchase a given debt security may instead accept a sufficiently high rating from a recognized rating agency. For creditworthy companies, the result may be a substantial savings in funding costs.
3. Outstanding rating opinions enable issuers to come to market quickly with new issues. In a market with many ratings outstanding, a rated issuer has a benchmark against which he can readily assess investor demands for pricing of debt rated at his level. Also, since investors have already been informed of the issuer's credit level, they will require less lead time before deciding to buy the new issue.

In more-developed credit markets, the "market access" value of ratings should translate into real economic value for issuers of debt. Thus, provided it can demonstrate that it has the confidence of a broad range of investors, a rating agency's largest source of revenues will be rating fees charged to issuers.

Value to Investment Bankers

Merchant bankers and other intermediaries who underwrite securities find ratings useful in the pricing, marketing, and placement of debt securities on behalf of their clients for such reasons as:

1. Ratings may help to open their client's new issues to a broader investor base.
2. The existence of a pool of rated debt securities may help to create a risk-based price structure in the market, which would enhance the underwriter's ability to judge the returns that investors are likely to demand on a new issue of a given credit quality.
3. Ratings also help intermediaries to monitor the risk and pricing of securities that are held temporarily in their own portfolios, either on behalf of clients or for trading on their own accounts.

Value to Regulators

Financial market regulators find that an independent rating system can be a factor in promoting stability and efficiency in the capital markets.

1. The transparency promoted by ratings allows for easier communication between issuers and investors, which can help to open up a cost-efficient means of financing to the nation's private-sector business.
2. A system of ratings that is publicly available and is prudently and continuously updated can help to counteract the effects of rumors and speculation, thereby lending added stability to the marketplace.

3. In Japan, the United Kingdom, and the United States, regulators use ratings to assign values to securities held in inventory under risk-based capital guidelines for securities dealers.
4. Overall, a well-run rating agency system may serve a number of quasi-regulatory market functions at less cost to government—for example, promoting a prudent investment decisionmaking process by investors.

A Brief Survey of the Rating Agency Industry
In Selected More-Developed Markets

Two types of rating agencies have emerged in more-developed credit markets: those that are international in scope and those that confine their rating judgments to local market issuers. (Generally, only local investors will rely on the rating opinions of rating agencies with local market content). For example, Moody's is an international rating agency that, over the last ten or more years, has expanded its coverage of international issuers, a reflection of the globalization of the capital markets. In addition to its New York headquarters, Moody's now has rating agencies in Tokyo, London, Paris, and Sydney. Conversely, the rating agencies in Australia, Canada, and France only rate local issuers.

The major source of rating agency revenues is derived from rating issuers of debt. Some rating agencies, such as Moody's, derive their fees for those ratings from the issuers themselves, and these agencies make their ratings publicly available to the marketplace, while others only make their ratings available to fee-paying subscribers. And some rating agencies will mix the two approaches. Moody's believes that by making its ratings available to the market as a whole stability and efficiency are promoted.

Rating agencies have been established in various developed credit markets around the world to meet the needs of both local and international market participants. In general, investor demand for credit ratings and research tends to vary among different capital markets, depending on the level of efficiency of the market and the institutionalization of the use of ratings in investor decisionmaking. A capital market is said to be efficient when securities prices reflect all available information on particular companies or securities. Demand for rating agency services is clearly the greatest in the United States, where the first rating agencies in the world were established at the beginning of the century.

Historically, investor demand for rating agency services has been fostered by issuer defaults. For example, until the close of the 1920s, ratings were viewed largely as adjuncts to Moody's financial publications. During the Great Depression, however, circumstances changed dramatically; the high incidence of bond defaults prompted demand for reliable, third-party opinions of credit quality. In another more recent example, the need for credit ratings on commercial paper was dramatically underscored by Penn Central Transportation Corporation's 1970 commercial paper default. Ratings are also regularly used in investor decisionmaking today in Australia, Canada, France, Germany, Japan, Switzerland, and the United Kingdom. Investors in these markets are served by a combination of local and international rating agencies.

There are many factors driving demand for rating agency services today, including the globalization of the world's capital markets, as well as the existence of new and often esoteric financial instruments, such as structured securities. Market participants around the world are expanding their horizons beyond national boundaries. In the process, technology is dissolving the barriers of distance, and information is being disseminated quicker and more efficiently. International investors have found that a borrower's name and size are no longer sufficient testimony to investment quality. Moreover, as the variety of debt securities grows and volatility becomes a fact of life, independent credit analysis is becoming a critical ingredient in sound portfolio management.

REFERENCES

Fry, Maxwell J. 1988. *Money, Interest, and Banking in Economic Development.* Baltimore: Johns Hopkins University Press.
World Bank. 1989. *The World Bank Development Report.* Washington, D.C.: World Bank.

9

Soviet–U.S. Joint Ventures: Problems, Challenges, and Opportunities

Keith A. Rosten

BACKGROUND

In January 1987, the Presidium of the Supreme Soviet issued an edict authorizing joint ventures between Soviet entities and foreign companies.[1] In accordance with this edict, the Soviet Council of Ministers adopted a decree (the "Joint Venture Decree") to enable Soviet and foreign entities to establish joint ventures within the Soviet Union.[2] The purported purpose of the Joint Venture Decree was to encourage closer cooperation between western companies and Soviet entities. Specifically, the Council of Ministers envisioned that this joint cooperation would: (1) satisfy Soviet requirements for certain industrial products, raw materials, and foodstuffs; (2) attract foreign technology, management experience, and material and financial resources; (3) develop the export base of the country; and (4) reduce unnecessary imports.[3]

In the wake of the Joint Venture Decree, many western companies began seriously to consider entering the Soviet market. As of

A version of this paper appears in the *California Management Review*, vol. 33, no. 2 (Winter 1991).

1. Edict of the Presidium of the Supreme Soviet adopted January 13, 1987, *Vedomosti SSR* (1987), No. 2, Item 35.
2. For commentary on and discussion of the Joint Venture Law, see Hobér (1989); Golubov (1989); Kashin (1989); and *Guide to Joint Ventures in the USSR* (New York: ICC Publishing Corporation, 1988).
3. Decree of the Council of Ministers adopted January 13, 1987, No. 49; *Sobranie postanovlenii pravitel'stva SSSR* (1987), No. 9, Item 40.

January 1990, the Ministry of Finance has registered over 1,200 joint ventures, of which approximately 140 have a U.S. partner.[4] The number of registered joint ventures is expected to double by the end of 1990.

The majority of the joint ventures reportedly has faltered; many have not and will not commence operations.[5] These ventures, similar to new businesses in the United States, are likely to experience a low rate of success, especially considering that the new ventures must operate in a foreign environment subject to the vagaries of the Soviet market, law, and politics. As a Ministry of Finance official expressed to me, the results of the joint venture legislation, especially joint ventures with U.S. companies, have been disappointing.

Soviet legislation governing Soviet joint ventures has been highly adaptable to a changing environment, but it leaves open many questions of interpretation (see Voznesenskaia 1988). Unfortunately, however, the legislation has been subject to change with little or no warning, sometimes challenging the fundamental assumptions underlying a joint venture. The Supreme Soviet is reportedly considering a comprehensive overhaul of the joint venture legislation. The major governing legislation is set forth below.

The Joint Venture Decree, adopted on January 13, 1987, was the seminal decree embracing the joint venture form for cooperative business ventures. It articulated the purposes underlying the enactment of the legislation, established the joint venture as a separate juridical person authorized to contract with others, and required the parties jointly to submit to the Ministry of Finance the joint venture agreement, the joint venture bylaws, and a feasibility study. The decree required that the joint venture be self-supporting, and it established a two-year tax holiday, after which the profits would be taxed at 30 percent.[6]

---

4. "Strangled by Red Tape," *The Economist*, 314 (7643), February 24, 1990, p. 72.

5. "Big Deals Run Into Big Trouble in the Soviet Union," *Business Week*, March 19, 1990, p. 58. *Business Week* reports that only about 18 percent of the registered joint ventures are operating.

6. After recent amendments, the two-year tax holiday now commences only after a "declared profit." Ministry of Finance Regulation, No. 226, November 30, 1987, amending Ministry of Finance Regulation, No. 124, May 4, 1987, Para. 15.

The Central Committee of the Communist Party of the Soviet Union and the Council of Ministers adopted a decision on September 17, 1987 (the "September 1987 Decree"), to simplify existing procedures to establish joint ventures.[7] The major change was to eliminate the necessity for approvals from numerous ministries and the Council of Ministers. Recognizing that exports from joint ventures had not materialized, the Central Committee and the Council of Ministers sought to promote exports by allowing, among other things, joint ventures to maintain their own freely convertible currency.

The December 2, 1988, Decree of the Council of Ministers (the "December 1988 Decree") marked a watershed in Soviet trade.[8] The decree enabled any enterprise, association, production cooperative, or other organization "whose products (works, services) are competitive on foreign markets" to engage in export-import operations.[9] The December 1988 Decree also allowed the joint venture to spend 10 percent of freely convertible currency on consumer goods; established a new customs tariff; enabled foreigners to occupy the chairmanship or general directorship of the venture; established that the joint venture could determine issues concerning hiring employees, salaries, and discharging employees; and allowed the foreigner to own a majority share of the venture.

The March 7, 1989, Decree of the Council of Ministers (the "March 1989 Decree") restricted the joint venture's export transactions to the joint venture's "own products and services" and allowed import only for the joint venture's "own needs."[10] The March 1989 Decree also outlined procedures relating to customs and duties. As the December 1988 Decree broadened the authority of joint ventures to engage directly in foreign trade, the March 1989 decree restricted the joint venture's foreign trade activities. On December 11, 1989, the Supreme Soviet adopted yet another decree (the "December 1989 Decree") imposing licensing requirements and

7. Decree of the Council of Ministers, No. 1074, September 17, 1987, *Svod zakonov SSSR* (1986 & Supp.), No. 9, pp. 50-28 - 50-34.
8. Decree of the Council of Ministers adopted December 2, 1988, No. 1405, *Sobranie postanovlenii pravitel' stva SSSR* (1989), No. 2, Item 7.
9. December 1988 Decree, Para. 2.
10. Decree of the Council of Ministers adopted March 7, 1989, No. 203, *Biulleten' Normativnykh Aktov Ministerstv i Vedomstv SSSR* (1989), No. 9, pp. 17-21.

quotas on exports of consumer goods and raw materials.[11]

In the wake of the Joint Venture Decree, the Soviet government has deemphasized direct purchases and turnkey operations and encouraged the formation of joint ventures. Since 1987, the Soviet side has generally urged some form of joint venture. The nature of the relationship depends on the respective goals and bargaining positions of the parties. The legislative fabric and other considerations heavily encourage Soviets to urge the joint venture form of doing business for several reasons.

First, Soviets view a joint venture with a foreign investor as an entrée to privileges reserved for the "elite," including travel abroad and access to foreign currency. Second, the joint venture structure also enables the venture to earn tax-free profits for at least two years. Third, the government does not assign any planning tasks to the joint venture. Finally, the joint venture can independently make decisions regarding salaries and hiring and firing of employees. Consequently, the Soviet partner is keenly interested in the joint venture alternative.

Because of these incentives, Soviets oftentimes may try to latch on to any western partner to obtain capital and to reap the benefits of the joint venture legislation. One Soviet representative candidly shared with me that the only purpose he had in forming a joint venture was to gain these benefits, and that he had little interest in the opinions or expertise of his western partner. Anxious to enter the Soviet market, the western partner often acquiesces to the joint venture structure, even recognizing that the joint venture under consideration may merely be a "fictitious marriage."

PURPOSE OF THE STUDY

The purpose of the study was to probe two fundamental aspects of joint ventures: negotiations and operations. The first segment of the study identified the major issues that the U.S. partner deemed important and those issues that were difficult to resolve during the

---

11. Decree of the Supreme Soviet, No. 1104, adopted December 11, 1989. This decree is discussed in "O regulirovanii vneshneekonomicheskoi deiatel'nosti v 1990 godu," *Sotsialisticheskaia Industriia*, December 24, 1989, p. 2.

course of the negotiations. The second segment of the study probed
the major hurdles that the joint ventures had to overcome to commence operations.
   It is estimated that fewer than 40 of the 140 Soviet-U.S. joint ventures are operating. I attempted to interview as many of the operational Soviet-U.S. joint ventures as possible. I was successful in in-
terviewing representatives (the "respondents") of sixteen joint ventures (the "responding joint ventures"), or almost one-half of the
operational Soviet-U.S. joint ventures. Most of the interviews took
place in Moscow. The respondents were from both the Soviet
Union and the United States.[12]

PROFILE OF RESPONDENTS

The responding joint ventures operate primarily in the service industries, though some of the responding joint ventures engage in
or plan to expand into manufacturing. The study obtained a good
distribution between older and more recent joint ventures.
Fourteen percent of the respondents were registered in 1987; 47
percent in 1988; and 39 percent in 1989. None of the U.S. partners
in the responding joint ventures owns a majority share in the
joint venture. Before the December 1988 Decree, the U.S. partner
could not own a majority share. But even in those joint ventures
registered after December 1988, the U.S. partner either ceded majority ownership to the Soviet partner or agreed to an equal share.
In 81 percent of those joint ventures participating in the study, the
Soviet partner owns a majority share; in 19 percent, the Soviet and
U.S. partners own equal shares.
   The parties to the joint venture capitalize the joint venture by
way of contributions to the joint venture's "charter fund." The contributions may take the form of buildings, equipment, the right to
use land, patents, and cash, among other things. Among the responding joint ventures, the U.S. partner invariably contributed
hard currency and sometimes proprietary processes. The Soviet

12. Complete survey results are not included due to space constraints. If you would
like more information on the study, please contact the author at Accord Consulting
Group, 444 Castro Street, Suite 400, Mountain View, CA 94041.

partner contributed rubles; 25 percent even contributed hard currency. Fifty percent of the Soviet partners contributed the right to use land or buildings.

Only 25 percent of the responding joint ventures have obtained financing for their operations. Most of the responding joint ventures have not attempted to obtain financing because they correctly assume that they would encounter substantial resistance from lenders to finance their fledgling enterprises.

Even in those instances in which the joint venture obtained financing, the U.S. partner generally loaned the money or guaranteed the loan. The lender looks to the credit of the western partner because the joint venture has neither a track record nor any hard assets for security. This lack of available financing hinders the growth prospects of joint ventures.

Soviet labor is inexpensive compared to western labor. The major disadvantage, however, is that Soviet labor is inefficient. The ability to harness and utilize this labor pool can be a critical competitive advantage for joint ventures.

The responding joint ventures collectively represent over 1,400 employees, of which 97 percent are Soviet. Although the study included a broad range of sizes for the joint ventures, ranging from three to over 700 employees, 50 percent of the joint ventures have fewer than 25 employees, 31 percent have 25 to 75 employees, and 19 percent have over 75 employees.

Less than 1 percent of the Soviets have received any training in the West. Several of the respondents indicated, however, that their respective joint ventures plan to provide training for some of their Soviet employees in the West.

STRUCTURES TO EARN HARD CURRENCY

The major incentive for the U.S. partner is to receive a distribution from the joint venture—in freely convertible currency. The major lever of success, therefore, is the joint venture's ability to generate hard currency, thereby allowing the U.S. partner to repatriate a hard currency profit. Accordingly, each venture must formulate a structure under which the joint venture generates more hard currency than it expends. There are several mechanisms that the venture can utilize to earn hard currency. These are discussed in detail below.

Serve the Soviet Market for Hard Currency

Within the Soviet Union, there are two primary means to earn hard currency: (1) sell to Soviet entities holding hard currency, or (2) sell to foreign businesses with operations in the Soviet Union.

An increasing number of Soviet state enterprises receive allocations of or earn hard currency. Cooperatives and other nonstate entities also can engage in exporting activities in accordance with the December 1988 Decree. Over 12,000 have registered to engage in foreign trade, though only a few of these realistically generate any hard currency.[13]

The joint venture can endeavor to sell its products or services to these Soviet customers for hard currency. The typical arrangement is to sell the products or services for a hard currency and a ruble component.

The foreign community in the Soviet Union needs a variety of products and services, many of which are not available or are difficult to obtain for rubles. Joint ventures have leaped into the void, offering food, lodging, transportation, and office support, among other services, for hard currency.

Wait for Ruble Convertibility

In addition, a few large companies are generating large amounts of rubles, reinvesting in other activities within the Soviet Union, expecting that the ruble will eventually become convertible. Some multinational companies have the wherewithal to remain in the Soviet market for a long time without repatriating profits. The Soviet market is simply a market that a large company cannot ignore. These companies take a farsighted view, and they want to be well-positioned when the ruble becomes convertible.

13. See *Wall Street Journal*, March 6, 1990, p. A-12.

Increase Business Opportunities for the U.S. Partner

Some U.S. companies do not expect to earn hard currency from the joint venture. Rather, they engage in the joint venture for the increased opportunities to their own business. For example, the U.S. company might enter into an exclusive dealing arrangement, under which the joint venture sells all the products that it produces to the U.S. partner. In this way, the U.S. company is effectively developing a supplier. Under a similar arrangement, the U.S. company may receive hard currency for services rendered to the joint venture. In this scenario, the U.S. company is developing a customer.

In either of these examples, the U.S. partner enters the joint venture for the increased business opportunities to the partner, and not for the profit potential of the joint venture itself. The profit that the western partner derives is from its increased business, not from repatriating a profit from the joint venture.

Countertrade

There are various methods of countertrade. In its classic form, the joint venture earns as many rubles as possible. Then the joint venture purchases goods that are marketable in the West—raw materials, for example. The joint venture sends these goods abroad and earns hard currency. Up until the March 1989 Decree, many joint ventures earned substantial amounts of rubles, purchased raw materials or other commodities for which there was a readily available market in the West, and sold the raw materials abroad. The March 1989 Decree, however, substantially eliminated this kind of arrangement, without a special dispensation from the Council of Ministers.

Serve the Foreign Market

The Soviet government has strongly attempted to encourage joint ventures to produce products for export. The joint venture earns all of its revenue in hard currency abroad. The export potential that the authors of the Joint Venture Decree envisioned has not been realized for several reasons. First, as little as 7 to 8 percent of Soviet goods meet western quality standards (see Shmelev 1987). Second, the Jackson-Vanik Amendment[14] imposes substantial tariffs on Soviet goods imported into the United States. Finally, western companies are not inclined to develop a producing capability in the Soviet Union that may cannibalize the market served by western operations.[15]

NEGOTIATIONS

Negotiations in the Soviet Union are not a sport for the short-winded. They are an arduous process, often leading to an unsuccessful result. Soviet and western parties have reportedly signed as many as 15,000 letters of intent, but they have discontinued the process because of disagreements during negotiations. Only about 2,400 Soviet-western joint ventures will have been registered by the end of 1990.

The joint ventures surveyed apparently represent a small minority in which the negotiations proceeded without major disagreements. But even the responding joint ventures required one year on average from the time they started searching for a partner until the joint venture was registered: four months to find a partner, six months of negotiations, and two months for the registration process. This one-year process does not even include further delays after registration.

The U.S. representatives of the responding joint ventures were asked to rank on a five-point scale several issues that may have been important to the U.S. side before the negotiations commenced. The U.S. representatives attached the most importance to management and control issues. They viewed the authority to make decisions of primary importance. Moreover, those issues relating to what the U.S. partner must contribute and what it would receive for

14. United States Code, Title 19, Sec. 2432.
15. An area of good potential for joint ventures serving the foreign market is exporting technology from the Soviet Union. As the Soviet Union reduces expenditures for its military-industrial complex, the institutes that previously supported research with military application will devote more time and energy to technology with nonmilitary applications.

those contributions were of the same level of importance. Before the negotiations, the U.S. partners were not interested in operational issues, such as housing, quality assurance, and supply of materials.

The respondents also were asked to rank several issues that may have been difficult to resolve during the course of the negotiations. Both U.S. and Soviet respondents did not view the negotiating process as very difficult. As one U.S. respondent suggested, the negotiating process is "more an educational process," because the Soviets are inexperienced in western business negotiations. Despite the ease with which most issues were resolved during the course of negotiations, as discussed above, the negotiations lasted on average six months.

There are at least two possible explanations why the parties were able to resolve these issues with relative ease but nevertheless required six months to complete the negotiations. First, negotiations do not proceed continuously. Rather, because of the distance they are staggered to accommodate the negotiating parties. Second, some may argue that the parties are generally both inclined to resolve the issues as quickly as possible. The U.S. side is pliable because it is anxious to conclude a deal. The Soviet side is also anxious to conclude the deal, and, as one respondent indicated, the Soviet partner may view the final contract as the beginning of negotiations.

OPERATIONS

The responding joint ventures have achieved some measure of success, by the mere fact that they have been able to overcome substantial hurdles to commence operations. It was difficult, however, to quantify this level of success other than considering the subjective impressions of the respondents. The study attempted to obtain a measure of success based on the respondent's subjective assessment of the financial success of the joint venture. Respondents cited several reasons for the success the joint venture has already achieved. These responses generally fell into the following three broad categories: (1) external business factors, 44 percent; (2) internal business factors, 38 percent; and (3) inter-partner relations,

31 percent.[16]

The first category, external business factors, refers to those factors external to the business. The respondents choosing this factor view the venture's success as a function of the demand for the industry's products or services. The joint venture has succeeded because the partners recognized the need for the joint venture's products or services.

The second category, internal business factors, refers to the competitive advantages of the joint venture, including the quality of management and the joint venture's distinctive competencies. The respondents citing this factor view the joint venture's success as a function of the abilities of management or the joint venture's capabilities.

For most western businesses, the analysis would stop there. But for these joint ventures, there is a third critical success factor. The final category, inter-partner relations, refers to the ability of the respective partners to rely on, trust, and communicate with one another. Those respondents identifying this factor perceptively view the ability to work with one's partner as a key factor in the success of the venture. The ability to get along with one's partner looms as a critical factor in the joint venture's success.

Delays are an endemic part of the joint venture process. Over half of those giving a response indicated that they had experienced significant delays between registration and when the joint venture commenced operations. Forty percent of the responding joint ventures had experienced unexpected delays of over four months from registration.

Only 38 percent of the responding joint ventures are very satisfied with the working relationship between the partners. The U.S. and Soviet representatives of the responding joint ventures have already encountered many areas of disagreement. These disagreements may exact a toll on the operating performance of the venture. There were a number of recurring themes of disagreement between the U.S. and Soviet parties. The major areas of disagreement are: (1) partner roles; (2) personnel; (3) diversification;

16. The percentages refer to the percentage of respondents who mentioned the factor. The percentages equal more than 100 percent because of multiple responses.

and (4) reinvestment of profits. Each of these areas is discussed below.

Partner Roles

The U.S. respondents recognize the critical role that their Soviet
partners fill. The Soviet respondents do not attach the same importance to the U.S. personnel. The Soviet partner generally operates
under the Soviet model, under which the authority to run an enterprise is concentrated in the general director (see Conyngham
1982). Up until the December 1988 Decree, a Soviet was required to
be the general director of the joint venture. Even after this decree,
a Soviet general director is the predominant model.

Soviet managers do not appear to be attuned to participative management techniques prevalent in the West. Not surprisingly, several of the U.S. deputy general directors of the responding joint
ventures expressed frustration that they do not have input into the
decisionmaking process as might be allowed or encouraged at a
western company.

Many U.S. respondents complained of the Soviets' utter lack of
understanding of western management style and techniques.
According to many U.S. respondents, the Soviets view a business
plan as a waste of time. In the same vein, some of the U.S. respondents suggested that their Soviet counterparts have no business
skills, are more inclined to "wheel and deal," and cannot quickly
adapt to market changes.[17]

A U.S. respondent offered a reason for the Soviets' lack of respon-
siveness. He perceptively noted that the Soviet personnel have a
dual allegiance. He reports to the Soviet partner, which is generally a Soviet enterprise, and to the joint venture. He must assure
that his actions comport with the views and interests of the Soviet
partner before he takes any action on behalf of the joint venture.

The Soviet respondents referred to the western partner's lack of
sensitivity to political, economic, and cultural differences. The
western partner wants to operate as if it were in a western country,

---

17. Although the ability of management may be one of the most important factors
of success, none of the responding joint ventures has a rigorous training program.

which the Soviet respondents think is unrealistic. They often dismiss the western partner's suggestions because the western partner does not understand the ways of the Soviet system.

Personnel

The Soviet partner generally is responsible for hiring employees. The western partner sometimes cedes this authority to the Soviet partner; other times, the Soviet partner assumes this authority, irrespective of the western partner's input. One respondent recalled that a Communist Party member had been "foisted" on the joint venture, before the western partner was successful in "retiring" him. In general, however, the western partner seems to defer to the Soviet partner on hiring decisions.

Diversification

A serious source of disagreement is the strategic direction of the joint venture. The Soviet partner oftentimes wants to expand the activities of the joint venture into unrelated activities. The personnel of the Soviet partner view themselves as "experts" in the Soviet system, rather than in an industry, and sincerely believe that the joint venture is well-positioned to capitalize on emerging opportunities even in unrelated industries.

The western partner wants to resist the diversification for several reasons. First, it wants to minimize the risk and avoid overextending itself. Second, it is unfamiliar with other areas into which the Soviet partner wants to expand. Third, it wants to move slowly in this market, observing the extent to which the relationship with the Soviet partner develops. Finally, and possibly most importantly, it believes that companies that diversify into unrelated industries perform demonstrably worse than firms that compete in one industry.[18]

18. For an example of one U.S.-Soviet joint venture whose activities were "frozen" because of the partners' disagreement on whether or not to diversify, see Rosten (1990).

Reinvestment

Another area of disagreement is the extent to which the joint venture will distribute profits to the partners. Generally, the U.S. partner wants to start earning a return on its investment as soon as possible. It has contributed hard currency into the venture and expects the venture to generate a profit from which the U.S. partner will realize a return.

The Soviet partner, in contrast, wants to reinvest the profits into the venture to expand the venture's operations. The Soviet partner can achieve its goals from the ongoing operations of the venture, irrespective of the distribution of profit. The partners' employees earn high salaries relative to other Soviet salaries, they can travel abroad, and they have access to hard currency. In the Soviet view, distribution of profits unnecessarily constrains the activities of the venture.

In addition, the Soviet partner does not want to declare a profit because the two-year tax holiday commences from the date on which there is a "declared profit." The joint venture can postpone payment of taxes if the venture can increase expenses such as production funds or inventory, which are shown as expenses. The U.S. partner is not as concerned with delaying the declaration of a profit because delaying declaring a profit constrains the U.S. partner's ability to repatriate a profit and, in any event, the joint venture pays taxes in rubles.

In one of the responding joint ventures, the Soviet partner wanted to increase the capital contributions to the venture, purportedly because the venture was "too" successful. The Soviet partner was worried that a large profit would elicit government charges of profiteering. An increased capital contribution would artificially deflate the return on investment.

Operational Difficulties

Although the responding joint ventures have generally achieved some level of success, they have encountered some substantial difficulties since they were registered. Despite evaluating their joint ventures as successful, 43 percent of the respondents interviewed felt that the venture had underperformed their expectations.

Each of the respondents was asked to rank on a five-point scale the difficulties the joint venture may have encountered. The most severe problems that the responding joint ventures have encountered relate to the Soviet infrastructure: living arrangements for foreigners, space, and communications within the Soviet Union. Because of the dismal living conditions, it is difficult to attract well-qualified westerners to work in the Soviet Union. Many of the joint ventures had serious problems in hiring and retaining western personnel. Many recognized that the presence of western personnel in the joint venture facilitates the operations of the joint venture and maximizes the possibility of success. Unfortunately, the lack of living space comparable to living space in the West makes the Soviet Union a hardship post.

A problem of a similar magnitude has been the lack of office space. Even large, multinational companies have been confined to meager quarters. The severe shortage has allowed those entities controlling office space to command rents comparable to those in New York—if space is available. As discussed above, the Soviet partner often purports to contribute the use of space for the operations of the joint venture; but it is oftentimes unclear who controls the space, and space that the partner claims is available to the joint venture later becomes "unavailable."

Many joint ventures have solved communications abroad by obtaining an international line. But communications within the Soviet Union persist as a serious problem. Problems such as interrupted service, static on the telephone, and the lack of capacity to send facsimiles continue to plague communications within the Soviet Union.

The responding joint ventures have encountered moderate difficulties relating to access to information, supplies, and markets. Only a small minority of the responding joint ventures has a marketing plan or perform any marketing activities; rather, the majority simply assumes that a market exists. Accordingly, even though information is in precious short supply, the lack of information is not often critical to the planning of the joint venture.

The responding joint ventures have not encountered difficulties in reaching their respective markets. For those that market products or services outside the Soviet Union, market access does not present a problem. For those that market within the Soviet Union, the single most common reason that customers purchase the product is because the product is otherwise unavailable. Consequently, market access is not a problem within the Soviet Union either.

Joint ventures fall outside the confines of the planning system; nevertheless, obtaining materials or equipment has not posed a considerable problem for several reasons. Most of the joint ventures needing materials planned to obtain the materials from abroad or on the domestic market for hard currency. Those joint ventures that rely on supplies within the Soviet Union for rubles have encountered the greatest difficulty, but they generally have planned for the difficulties in obtaining materials.

Potential problems relating to importing, exporting, and customs have not posed severe difficulties for the responding joint ventures. The representatives of the responding joint ventures related creative ways by which they have adapted to the Soviet market and minimized these problems. One respondent, for example, recalled severe shipping delays by ship and train into the Soviet Union. Now the joint venture utilizes a trucking company. Another respondent related difficulty with customs, until the company hired a former customs official to work for them.

The responding joint ventures have not tried, or did not relate to me their attempts, to circumvent the bans on exporting raw materials imposed by the March 1989 Decree and the December 1989 Decree. They have not had difficulty in exporting their products from the Soviet Union.

The respondents have not occasioned any particular difficulty with customs, having received exemptions from customs for goods imported as part of the western partner's contribution to the joint venture. The December 1988 Decree stated that goods imported into the Soviet Union may be entitled to reduction or even exemption of customs duties.[19] Nevertheless, customs duties loom as a potential problem. The Soviet Union recently adopted a new customs tariff,[20] which applies with equal force to joint ventures. Unless the

---

19. See December 1988 Decree, Para. 4-6.
20. Customs regulations are considered secret and are not available to the general public.

joint venture obtains an exemption from these duties, importing may become a serious problem.

Banking has also posed a problem for the responding joint ventures. Joint ventures have been required to open their foreign currency accounts at Vneshekonombank, the Soviet bank that oversees foreign currency. The representatives of the responding joint ventures were not pleased with this monopoly over their banking relations. Check clearance can take as long as five weeks. Those accepting credit cards must pay very high fees to Intourist to process the paperwork. For those joint ventures engaged in retail businesses, there are severe restrictions on accepting cash.

The respondents attribute the problems that they have encountered to many different causes, the five most prevalent of which are: (1) shortages, 88 percent; (2) bureaucracy, 88 percent; (3) restrictive legislation, 63 percent; (4) negotiations, 38 percent; and (5) management attention, 38 percent.[21] The implication is that good planning and selection of a strong and reliable partner can minimize the effect of the problems the joint ventures have encountered. The only source of problems that the joint venture cannot control or for which it cannot plan is restrictive legislation. Otherwise, the respondents recognized that, working with their respective partners, the joint venture can substantially overcome the problems enumerated earlier.

AREAS OF PROPOSED LEGISLATIVE CHANGES

Some respondents were dubious that any legislative change would foster the kinds of changes that would better facilitate the operations of joint ventures. As one respondent stated, "the cultural problems far outweigh legislative considerations. People don't respond to legislation." These respondents attached paramount importance to the problems associated with the economy, culture, and politics, and they minimized the effect that legislative change might have.

---

21. The percentages refer to the percentage of respondents that mentions the factor as a source of problems. The percentages equal more than 100 percent because of multiple responses.

There are over twenty decrees governing joint ventures in the Soviet Union, many of which are unpublished or published in excerpted form. Several decrees conflict with one another or other Soviet legislation, making compliance difficult to achieve. Also, the status of joint ventures remains uncertain until the Supreme Soviet adopts a comprehensive law governing joint ventures.

Several respondents raised concerns about the stability of the legislation and the effect of legislative changes on their operations. For example, Soviet customs officials refused to allow a ship belonging to a responding joint venture to set sail because of the new restrictions of the December 1989 Decree. After negotiations in Moscow, the ship was finally allowed to leave. The lack of stability does not foster an environment in which western businesses are confident that their investments are secure.

Many recommendations for legislative changes centered on efforts to provide an easier mechanism by which the western partner can repatriate profits until the ruble becomes convertible. There were several suggestions in this regard. One respondent suggested that there should be a guarantee of repatriation to the extent of one's investment. If a western company contributed US$1 million to a joint venture, and the venture performs well but earns only rubles, the western partner should be allowed to repatriate at least the ruble equivalent (at some set exchange rate) of US$1 million.

All of the respondents affected by restrictions on barter vociferously recommended lifting the barter restrictions introduced in the March 1989 Decree. While the March 1989 Decree was ostensibly a product of the Soviet government's negative response to exports of raw materials, it was more likely a concession to foreign trade organizations to assume greater control over barter arrangements. Nevertheless, this restriction has severely inhibited the ability of joint ventures to generate hard currency. Until the ruble becomes convertible, the Soviet government should promote arrangements to allow joint ventures to generate hard currency.

In addition, a new tax treaty between the United States and the Soviet Union would facilitate repatriation of profits.[22] The U.S.

22. The current bilateral tax treaty, which was signed June 20, 1973, and which became effective January 1, 1976, does not exempt the tax on repatriation of profits to the U.S. partner. Convention between the United States of America and the Union of Soviet Socialist Republics on Matters of Taxation, June 20, 1973.

company now must pay an additional 20 percent on that portion of the profit which is transferred abroad.[23] A new tax treaty would reduce this tax to zero.[24]

In a similar vein, the Soviets ban certain activities, such as exporting raw materials. Many of the respondents suggested that the Soviet government should impose higher taxes on activities it wants to discourage but not impose outright bans.

The joint ventures have been able to maintain foreign currency accounts only at Vneshekonombank. Several respondents were concerned that this restriction constrained their ability to develop banking relationships with other western banks, from which they could seek financing. Relaxing this monopoly might promote a competitive spirit, resulting in more efficient operations. In addition, currency restrictions severely disable those retail businesses serving the foreign community in Moscow and other Soviet cities. Joint ventures should be allowed to accept hard currency in cash.[25]

The respondents identified four areas ripe for legislative change in the U.S.: (1) lifting restrictions on technology transfers; (2) allowing more visas to Soviet citizens; (3) waiving the Jackson-Vanik Amendment; and (4) adopting a new tax treaty. The tax treaty was discussed above. The other areas are discussed below.

Technology Transfer

The Coordinating Committee on Multilateral Export Controls, known as COCOM, of which the United States is a member, controls strategic exports to various countries, including the Soviet Union. COCOM formulates detailed lists of embargoed commodities and technical data that are strategically significant. But many COCOM member nations routinely violate the restrictions; and in light of the prevailing political environment, many restrictions

23. Joint Venture Decree, Para. 41. The December 1988 decree provides for some tax concessions on a case-by-case basis.
24. The Soviet and U.S. governments are reportedly negotiating a new tax treaty.
25. The respondents also related views on areas for change in Soviet domestic legislation. They suggested changes in housing legislation; private ownership so that the joint venture can own buildings and land; and taxes so that local authorities could reap some of the benefits of joint ventures operating in their geographic areas.

are outdated. The respondents agreed that COCOM's rigid restrictions inhibit the development of Soviet trade and disenable joint ventures from providing the same level of service or the same quality of products as one would find in the West.

Visas

The United States has imposed a quota, severely restricting the number of extended visas to Soviets coming to the United States for commercial representation. Hence, it is difficult for Soviets to remain in the United States for extended periods of time. For joint ventures wanting their Soviet personnel to remain in the United States for extended periods, this restriction is a major obstacle.

Jackson-Vanik Amendment

All agreed that the Jackson-Vanik Amendment should be waived. The U.S. Congress enacted this amendment primarily to promote emigration from the Soviet Union. Jackson-Vanik withheld most favored nation status from the Soviet Union until the Soviet Union liberalized emigration. As the Soviet Union has substantially liberalized emigration over the past year, the Jackson-Vanik Amendment should be waived.

RECOMMENDATIONS

The Soviet experience with joint ventures is in its nascent stage of development. Soviet legislation reflects the political debate on the necessary steps to facilitate the Soviet Union's integration into the world economy and the pace at which these steps should be implemented. The responding joint ventures are in essence the pioneers at the forefront of this great experiment, recognizing that the potential rewards may be commensurate with the risk. Based on the experience of the responding joint ventures, other western companies can enhance the possibility of success by observing eight basic rules:

1. Be forever vigilant of cultural differences.
2. Consider alternative cooperation agreements.
3. Closely examine the prospective partner.
4. Structure the agreement to respond to both parties' needs.
5. Proceed only with a sound business strategy.
6. Create an effective means to repatriate profits.
7. Assure western personnel an active role in operations.
8. Plan around deficiencies and shortages.

For the company considering entering the Soviet market, these rules are prerequisites to the success of its enterprise. Each of these rules is discussed below.

Be Sensitive to Differences with the Soviet Union

The Soviet Union is an enormous country with vast natural resources, inexpensive labor, and areas of technological advancement. But for the western partner to tap the Soviet Union's potential, it must recognize and incorporate into its strategy the cultural, political, and economic differences that the Soviet Union presents. These differences will permeate the entire project. The ability to address these differences is key to a successful enterprise.

Evaluate Alternative Cooperation Agreements

The Soviet Union is placing considerable emphasis on joint venture agreements. Even if the western party perceives that a simple purchase and sale agreement might fill its needs, the western company is likely to encounter considerable resistance from the Soviet entity because of the substantial benefits that the Soviet partner can reap under a joint venture structure, including foreign travel, access to hard currency, lower tax rates, more flexibility in labor relations, and no planning tasks.

Soviet partners have sometimes lured western companies into a relationship that the western company neither needs nor wants. Although the Soviets admit their need for western expertise, often times the particular Soviet partner is merely searching for capital, not western management skills. The form of a joint venture provides an expedient mechanism to achieve its goals.

The western partner must weigh the incentives that the joint venture legislation offers with the risks of engaging in a joint venture in terms of time, energy, and capital. Depending on the bargaining position of the parties, a Soviet entity may still be amenable to entering into more traditional forms of cooperation.

Select the Appropriate Partner

The selection of the partner represents the single most important determinant of success of the venture, especially in cases of joint ventures. The western partner should choose a partner who can work with western personnel and facilitate operations in the Soviet Union. The western partner must specifically evaluate the prospective partner's authority, abilities, agenda, and trustworthiness long before it ever signs a joint venture agreement.

Some prospective partners may represent that they have the authority to perform certain functions. A quick review of their charters may show that they are not entitled to do what they say they can do. Some Soviet entities have a substantial track record. In contrast, many cooperatives recently commenced operations, and their capabilities are difficult to judge. Moreover, the legislation governing cooperatives is in flux and will reportedly be substantially revised. In any event, the authority of the prospective partner must be thoroughly researched.

Even if a prospective partner has the authority, it still may not have the ability to pilot the project through the Soviet system. Contacts with ministerial officials and connections with local officials are essential to get things through the system. The western partner must attempt to analyze the track record or other relevant data to determine whether the prospective partner has the ability and capability to discharge its responsibilities under the joint venture agreement.

The western partner must evaluate what benefits the Soviet partner intends to reap from the joint venture. A hidden agenda can have a debilitating effect on the venture's operations. Some Soviets candidly related to me that they did not care to what kind of venture they became attached—just so long as they could spend time in the United States. Determining the agenda of the prospective partner can be a particularly challenging endeavor, but the western partner must attempt to identify the Soviet partner's goals.

Finally, the trustworthiness of the prospective partner is critical. Many of the responding joint ventures referred to their relationships as corporate marriages. The western partner must be certain that the Soviet partner will devote the time and resources to the venture and not contravene the agreement. The western partner may structure the agreement to make incremental contributions contingent on the Soviet partner's performance under the agreement. Although there may not be other objective ways to determine the trustworthiness of the partner, the western partner must keep this issue firmly in mind.

Structure the Agreement to Meet the Needs of the Parties

The western partner should recognize that the parties are operating under an entirely different set of values. Their goals may be very different but reconcilable. The western partner may want to repatriate hard currency profits; the Soviet partner may want to gain access to western goods and travel abroad. This divergence of goals may be the source of frustration and tension, but it also creates the possibility for creative approaches to help both parties achieve their respective goals. The parties should structure the joint venture so that both parties can achieve their goals.

There remains at least one major area that requires particular attention: control of decisions. The percentage of ownership is not as important as the control over certain decisions. The western partner must enumerate in the joint venture documents those critical decisions over which it wants to retain control. The Soviets are generally legalistic and will abide by the provisions in the joint venture agreement. But the agreement must be clear and unambiguous.

The parties should also keep in mind that even if their approach
may not comport entirely with the governing joint venture legislation, the Ministry of Finance can and will extend concessions and
grant special dispensations, depending on the particularities of the
joint venture.

Formulate a Sound Business Strategy

Many of the responding joint ventures have performed well because they have faced little or no competition. They recognize that
the primary reason their customers have retained their services or
purchased their products is because there has been no alternative.
The opening of the Soviet market, however, will bring increased
competition. The best way to succeed in a competitive market is to
develop a business strategy under which the joint venture is able to
sustain a competitive advantage.

The Soviets, untrained in western management techniques, may
consider that planning is a waste of time, that the parties have already "jointly" prepared a financial feasibility study, and that further planning is unnecessary. Business planning is a fundamental aspect of all businesses. It forces management to grapple with
financing, operations, marketing, and organizational issues. The
feasibility study is for the Ministry of Finance, and it is not intended as a planning document. Thus, it is woefully inadequate as
a planning tool. The partners should prepare a sound business
plan, formulating a strategy for the company and addressing how
the functional areas will contribute to achieving the joint venture's
strategy.

A joint review of these issues will minimize the risk of disagreement over fundamental aspects of the venture, such as diversification. The western partner should confine the activities of the
venture to a specific business purpose, on which the parties have
agreed before embarking on the venture. Diversification will lead
to poor results. As one U.S. business professor has observed, "[M]ost
diversification fails. Many companies lack a clear concept of corporate strategy to guide their diversification. . . . Others fail because
they implement a strategy poorly" (Porter 1987). Based on this
sound policy, the parties should focus their energies on one busi-

ness rather than starting multiple unrelated businesses simultaneously.[26]

Formulate and Agree on a Structure to Repatriate Any Profit

For the western partner, the primary motivation is eventually to repatriate a hard currency profit. The parties must recognize that hard currency is the primary lever for the joint venture, without which the venture will not succeed. This consideration presents the risk that the parties will not agree on how to allocate hard currency revenues and whether to reinvest or disburse profits.

The parties should specifically address this point before entering into the joint venture agreement. For example, they can prioritize the uses to which they will put hard currency revenues, or they can use a payout ratio for hard currency. In any event, the western partner must have a certain comfort level that once the joint venture earns hard currency, the western partner will be able to repatriate some of that hard currency.

Assume an Active Role in Operations

The presence of western personnel is critical for the western partner to maintain some control over the operations of the joint venture—unless the western partner is content to be a silent partner. Western personnel can inculcate western values into the organization and train the Soviets to assume greater responsibility. Soviet managers should come to the United States to receive additional training.

Soviet managers may resist this change because it is a change. But the role of the westerner should be secured in the agreement. The Soviet model under which the power is concentrated in a supreme general director is not relevant in a joint venture. The general director should not wield autocratic power. The westerner must have actual influence.

---

26. Sound business policy, however, may require more backwards integration than one would expect in the West due to shortages in the Soviet economy.

Formulate an Operations Plan Taking into Consideration the Particularities of the Soviet System

The Soviet market poses a particular challenge for the operations plan of the joint venture. The parties to the joint venture should anticipate and attempt to plan for expected deficiencies in the Soviet economy. The western partner should disabuse itself of any notion that it can rely on the same supplies, services, and facilities that it can obtain in the West. Indeed, a strong and reliable Soviet partner will be able to reduce the problems. Nevertheless, contingency planning, especially in the areas of facilities, housing arrangements, and supply lines, is essential.

CONCLUSION

The fundamental political changes in East Europe have brought a new day for capitalism in the Soviet market. This market presents tremendous opportunities, offering a wealth of natural resources, inexpensive labor, some areas of advanced technology, and a market of 290 million consumers. A Bush administration official recently predicted that trade with the Soviet Union will increase to as much as US$15 billion in the next several years.[27]

As U.S. companies seek to capitalize on these opportunities, they should recognize that penetrating this market is a tortuous road fraught with uncertainties and instability. Those choosing to enter the Soviet market should expect to encounter substantial hurdles. Even a small project can exact a heavy toll on the energies of the most perseverant western partner. For those that endure and observe the eight fundamental rules outlined above, however, the rewards should be substantial.

---

27. "Annual Trade With Soviets Could Reach As Much As $15 Billion, Bush Aide Says," *Wall Street Journal,* February 8, 1990, p. 3.

REFERENCES

Conyngham, William J. 1982. *The Modernization of Soviet Industrial Management.* New York: Cambridge University Press.

Golubov, G. D., ed. 1989. *Sovmestnye predpriiatiia, mezhdunarodnye obedineniia i organizatsii na territorii SSSR.* Moscow: Yuridicheskaia literatura.

Hobér, Kaj. 1989. *Joint Ventures in the Soviet Union.* Dobb's Ferry, N.Y.: Transnational Juris Publications, Inc.

Kashin, Vladimir, 1989. *Rubl' + dollar.* Moscow: Molodaia gvardiia.

Porter, Michael. 1987. "From Competitive Advantage to Corporate Strategy." *Harvard Business Review,* Vol. 65, No. 3, May-June.

Rosten, Keith A. 1990. "Soviet Joint Ventures Riding on Troubled Waters." *Wall Street Journal,* May 7, p. A 14.

Shmelev, N. 1987. "Avansy i dolgi." *Novy Mir,* Vol. 63, No. 6, June, p. 154.

Voznesenskaia, N. 1988. "Sovmestnye predpriiatiia s uchastiem firm kapitalisticheskikh i razvivaiushchikhsia stran na territorii SSSR." *Sovetskoe i pravo,* No. 1, p. 125.

10

The Positive Influence of Legal Reform on Soviet–U.S. Joint Ventures

Viktor P. Mozolin

INTRODUCTION

Joint ventures with foreign capital will figure prominently in the economic system based on diverse property forms that are being considered as part of the radical economic reform in the Soviet Union. It is impossible at this point to predict the proportions of joint ventures and foreign companies in the future industrial structure of the Soviet Union. The data on the numbers of currently registered joint ventures and the size of their authorized capital do not give any insight either.[1] The reasons why the success of Soviet joint ventures has been rather modest to date are common knowledge. Although the Soviet state favors foreign investment and seeks to encourage it, the country's economy, still under the control of administrative-command management methods, remains unresponsive to those forms of business based on market relations. Another factor is the slow pace of radical economic reform, particularly of the steps intended to introduce the convertibility of the ruble. As a result, foreign companies, in particular large ones, prefer to adopt a wait-and-see policy.

The economic reform under way in the Soviet Union is quite unusual. It seeks to replace an economic management system based on the administrative-command method of economic management

---

1. As of January 1, 1990, there were 1,274 registered joint ventures, with an aggregate authorized capital of 3.3 billion rubles. At present, their total number is approaching 2,000.

115

with a totally different one, in which the national economy would be built along entirely different lines. This is not a problem of quantitative change in the economy, rather it is a qualitative transition from one state of the economy to another. This is why perestroika in the Soviet Union is described as revolutionary and the economic reform as radical.

At present, the country is in the midst of a transition to a regulated market economy. At the same time the radical economic reform is taking place, the country is experiencing major political reform. In conformity with the Resolution of the 2nd Congress of People's Deputies of December 20, 1989, "On the Measures To Revitalize the Economy, the State of the Economic Reform and Policy Approaches Toward the Elaboration of the 13th Five-Year Plan," there are plans to gear the country toward market relations within the framework of a multistructured economy.

This multistructured economy shall be based on the state-run economy at three levels: (1) the All-Union economy, (2) the Union and autonomous republics' economy, and (3) the local economy, collective and individual. Mixed economic forms, including businesses with foreign capital, will be prominent in this multistructured economy. All of the above structures and forms of economic management should be seen as a single economic body. The proportions of each of the structures at every stage of economic development will change in response to the course of the reform and the extent to which the Soviet economy is integrated into the global market economy. Businesses established or operating with the participation of foreign capital on Soviet territory will become one of the most essential channels for gearing the Soviet national economy toward the world market. Such businesses will only be able to function if a market economy exists within the Soviet Union. Only in this case would these businesses and the other structures of the multistructured economy stand a realistic chance of success.

LEGAL PROBLEMS OF PERESTROIKA

The transition to a market economy in the Soviet Union is governed by laws. Because such a transition in the economic sphere has a radical character affecting virtually every aspect of Soviet society, the legal changes also must be sweeping and radical. This reform does not limit itself to a face-lift of individual laws, but rather it addresses deep-seated layers of Soviet legislation, leaving in force only those laws that are based on global values and that reflect the achievements of world and domestic legal practice. For example, many legal norms concerning purchases and sales that are contained in the Fundamentals of Civil Legislation of the Soviet Union and of the Union Republics and the Civil Codes of the Union Republics will be quite sufficient for the conditions of a market economy, all the more so as they are intended for this type of economy. At the same time, we will have to renounce those that were intended to ensure the functioning of the administrative-command economy and to limit the interests of buyers and consumers of goods purchased at state-owned shops.

The conduct of the radical legal reform entails a number of objective difficulties, as outlined below.

Problem Number 1

The legal reform has to be conducted in the face of the continued existence of the legislative and law-enforcement systems that took shape before perestroika. Therefore, every major law of market orientation that is adopted by the state comes into conflict with the legislation in force and with the existing system of enforcement, which often renders it toothless. For example, this has been the case with the Law on State Enterprise of 1987. The same is taking place with the new Law on Leases, which the Supreme Soviet adopted in late 1989. It is natural that the cause of the problems goes far beyond the juridical sphere of relations between individual laws. Behind every law there are certain social strata and state structures pursuing their own interests. The basic reason for the low efficiency of the Law on Leases at present is the opposition on the part of the existing ministries and departments controlling and supervising state enterprises and associations, the Ministry of Finance, and collective and state farms that are not interested in leasing out their property. The opposition reflects the functions that the state has assigned to these supervisory organizations. The efficiency of every new law depends on the results of the struggle between the old and new practices and on the broader struggle between the social forces standing for perestroika and those opposing it. This struggle starts at the lawmaking stage and, as a rule, results in the adoption of half-hearted, "band-aid" laws.

Problem Number 2

The laws constituting the core of the legal reform should be intended for the regulation of social and economic relations that do not exist at the time of the laws' adoption. These laws are intended to introduce new relations and forms in place of old ones, not to endorse the already existing economic relations and institutions. In this connection, the question is what kind of new relations are at stake, because legislation is capable of regulating specific, particular social relations, but not abstract ones. When working out economic legislation, lawmakers should be guided first by an accurate, scientifically well-grounded prognosis concerning the nature and parameters of the market to come into existence in the Soviet Union. What kind of market will it be? Will it be of the New Economic Policy type, one existing in the United States or Japan or Scandinavia or Poland, taking into account both its economic parameters and the distinguishing features of the emerging Soviet federation? Unfortunately, today one would be hard put to answer the question, though as a whole, the market structure has been outlined by the Resolution of the 2nd Congress of People's Deputies of December 20, 1989. It stands to reason that under such conditions the preparation of, say, a detailed law on competition and antitrust violations in the Soviet market is impossible. There are also some other equally important circumstances that should be taken into account. The new laws aimed at revolutionizing economic relations in society are intended to defend the interests of social strata and groups that cannot be regarded as the majority of the population at the moment of the adoption of these laws. In addition to the introduction of market relations, the radical legal reform will introduce changes in the Soviet Union's social structure. The more radical a law is, the greater is the opposition on the part of the social groups and state structures that have no future in the new type of socialist society being created through perestroika. The deputies in the current Supreme Soviet are required to show high responsibility in understanding the tasks before society and in accomplishing them when adopting laws.

Problem Number 3

The third problem concerns the action of the time factor. There are plans to work out and adopt, if possible, all the basic laws pertaining to the radical economic reform in 1990. This is a supremely challenging task, and it calls for large-scale efforts of many experts, including lawyers and deputies. Many of the laws, those regulating the capital markets, for example, are new. A fair number of laws have to be elaborated from scratch. It is very difficult to provide a professional level for these laws under such conditions, let alone to assure their passage through the Supreme Soviet, the deputies of which, representing different social strata of society, are quite sensitive to and have a high responsibility for each law they consider. Dealing with such responsibilities requires a lot of time. And, as is clear from the work experience of the three sessions of the new Supreme Soviet, the mechanism for the discussion and adoption of these laws has yet to be adequately worked out. As a result, the adopted laws sometimes contain conflicting legal norms and even entire provisions that need to be rescinded or at least suspended. Thus, the Soviet Law on Leases describes both the leaser's organizations and the leased enterprises under their control as juridical persons, though in the former case the law does speak of the subject of the law—that is, a juridical person—while in the latter case, only of the object of the law. With so many laws to be drafted and enacted, jurisprudence cannot keep abreast of the conceptual elaboration of the prepared laws, which reflects on their content and efficiency. Being alive to the uniqueness of the situation in which our country has found itself and to the attendant need to accelerate the adoption of new laws providing for the implementation of a radical economic reform, it is necessary to have a well-defined strategy for legal reform in the Soviet Union.

Problem Number 4

Many Union Republics have proclaimed the superiority of their
laws over the laws of the Soviet Union. This problem may be decided in the pending Union Treaty that is now being prepared.

THE STRATEGY OF RADICAL LEGAL REFORM

The legal reform of the economy is one of the most integral parts
of the general legal reform being conducted in the Soviet Union
within the framework of the construction of a rule-of-law state.
There are four basic schemes for the review of legislation to ensure
gearing the economy toward the new planned market management methods.

Scheme Number 1

Scheme Number 1 can be described as a "multiple legislation on
the basis of laws passed one by one." This scheme was tested in
practice and, taken as a whole, failed to acquit itself well. Its implementation began when the Law on Individual Labor Activities
was adopted in 1986; the Law on the State Enterprise in 1987; a
Decree of the Presidium of the Supreme Soviet; and two resolutions
of the Soviet Council of Ministers on joint ventures, even though
they, in particular the Law on Cooperatives, which was more oriented toward the market production than the other laws, failed to
produce the results for which their authors hoped.

   The basic reasons for the failure are: (1) the laws did not affect
the existing fundamentals of production relations, above all, the
property relations, and (2) the laws kept in force the current administrative-command system of economic management.

Scheme Number 2

Scheme Number 2 is referred to as a "system based on the fundamental general law and individual normative acts issued to specify

it," which envisages the adoption at the level of Soviet law of the general provisions concerning the management of the economy under the conditions of a transition to a market economy. Such general provisions would formulate the principles and norms regulating economic relations and determine the lines in the development of legislation within its specific terms of reference. Individual laws should be adopted to elaborate such general procedures as the laws on property, state enterprise, shareholder societies, and other kinds of companies, taxation, banks, and inventions.

This scheme is sensible, as it gives the lawmaker a chance to program his activities and, importantly, to adopt coordinated laws. But, as is obvious from the practical activities of the Supreme Soviet, it cannot be used per se because many laws pertaining to individual spheres of the economy have been adopted or are currently passing through the Soviet Parliament. To be sure, this does not rule out the possibility of the adoption of a comprehensive law while the legal reform is being implemented.

Scheme Number 3

Described as "Constitution first, then economic legislation," Scheme Number 3 is the most logical, yet it is very difficult to put into action. Many problems of the country's economic development will be addressed over the course of perestroika, and the outcome cannot be predicted as yet. This is one of the most distinguishing features of both the economic and political transformations under way in society. The legal reform has taken a different tack. The modification of the Soviet Constitution, or rather the ongoing formulation of a new one, is taking place concurrently with the adoption of new laws. This was the case with political legislation that witnessed the establishment of new bodies of state power and administration. The same changes are taking place in the sphere of the legal regulation of the economy, where property and other kinds of relations are undergoing fundamental change. In this connection, this scheme would better be described as the "Concurrent Development of the Constitution and of the Economic Legislation."

Scheme Number 4

Finally, Scheme Number 4, a direct continuation of Scheme Number 3, is called "bloc (package) legislation." At present, the Congress of People's Deputies and the Supreme Soviet use this system, and they assume that it works. Its essence is that the legislation concerning economic reform is adopted on a package-by-package basis. The package of the most essential economic laws is elaborated and adopted at the first stage as a basic priority. It includes laws on property, land, lease, taxation, enterprise, and the fundamentals of the management of the economy and the social sphere.

In conformity with the Resolution of the 2nd Congress of People's Deputies, the second package includes laws on the State Bank, the banking system, investment activities, employment, and other legislative acts connected with the implementation of the economic reform and the acceleration of scientific and technological progress. As is clear, the second package of the economic legislation covers virtually all of the remaining lawmaking concerning the transition of the country's economy to the market-oriented economic management methods. Significantly, the whole package of such laws should be elaborated and submitted to the Supreme Soviet in 1990. Time will show if the scheme is realistic, but it is clear even today that it would call for a huge effort on the part of those preparing the drafts of the above-mentioned and other laws, and, regrettably, it may take its toll on the quality of the legislation. It cannot be forgotten that we are dealing with the preparation of laws intended to regulate, in the overwhelming majority of cases, new, emerging social relations.

This gives rise to other essential questions for lawmakers to tackle: Should the proposed legislation cover only the period of transition to the market economy? Can it contain norms intended for use under the conditions of the already functioning market economy? Variant Number 1 is attractive in that it makes it possible to limit oneself to incorporating into the corresponding laws only the most basic provisions needed to make the old norms restraining the development of market relations in the country null and void. As far as the new norms are concerned, their regulatory functions can be minimized in this case. The transition to the market economy thus will be effected vigorously and on the basis of economic laws that are not weighted down by lawmakers' prescriptions. But this variant has the one essential flaw that, in the final analysis, is the reason why such an approach has been renounced: Under the present-day conditions, when the fundamentals of the administrative-command system of economic management have yet to be broken down, and political power is in the hands of the bureaucratic state and party apparatus, the vigorous movement toward the planned market economy would be accompanied by the growth of the role of administrative and departmental lawmaking, which may lead the Soviet Union down a blind alley.

This is why lawmaking in the economic field began to be based on an alternative variant connected with the elaboration and adoption of the laws to be used during the transition period and the period during which the Soviet Union's economy is geared toward the stable methods of its future development. To be sure, such a long-term sweep of the laws does not make it possible to envisage many details of the future economic relations in the legal norms introduced at the present stage. Thus, there will be a need to adjust such laws from time to time, which is a normal course in the development of lawmaking in all countries. In fact, a different aspect is important. There can be no mistake in the determination of goals, basic methods, and the parameters of the realization of these goals. The conceptual aspect of such laws is taking on increasing importance.

IMPLICATIONS FOR JOINT VENTURES

The lines in the conduct of legal reform, and the difficulties arising before it, fully apply to joint ventures established by Soviet and foreign organizations. In this case, a joint venture can be defined as the form of entrepreneurship with the participation of Soviet and foreign capital that is legal under Soviet law, not the legal form of organization as a juridical person engaged in such activities. But the legislation currently in force fails to make a distinction between the two concepts. In accordance with the Decree of the Supreme Soviet of January 13, 1987, the Ruling of the Council of Ministers No. 48 of January 13, 1987, and the Ruling of the Council of Ministers No. 49 of January 13, 1987, on joint ventures to be established on Soviet territory, the concept of a joint venture is used as a juridical person empowered to engage in a certain type of business. The Soviet Constitution and the body of civil laws regard an enterprise as the subject, not the object, of law. In the future, however, in connection with the forthcoming adoption of the Law on Shareholding Companies and Other Kinds of Business Partnerships, the concept of a joint venture will acquire genuine significance as a form of business activity, that is, as the object rather than the subject of law.

At present, in contrast to the United States and many other industrially developed capitalist countries that do not have a separate legislation regulating joint ventures, Soviet relations connected with the establishment and activities of joint ventures with the participation of foreign capital are regulated by two kinds of legal norms: special and general ones. Special legal norms are those that take priority over the general legal norms, and the latter are not used if the former exist. Paragraph 1 of the Ruling of the Council of Ministers "On the Procedure Regulating the Establishment on Soviet Territory of Joint Ventures with the Participation of Soviet Organizations and Companies of Capitalist and Developing Countries" says: "Joint ventures organize their activities in conformity with the Decree of the Presidium of the Supreme Soviet of the USSR of January 13, 1987, on matters connected with the establishment on Soviet territory and the activities of joint ventures, international associations and organizations with the participation of Soviet and foreign organizations, companies and administrative bodies, this ruling and other legislative acts of the Union of Soviet Socialist Republics and the Union Republics with exceptions laid down by the Soviet Union's interstate and intergovernmental treaties."

In a number of cases, the lawmaker cites the general legal norms. For example, in accordance with Paragraph 48 of the Ruling of the Council of Ministers of January 13, 1987, Soviet legal norms regulate the hours, labor conditions, fringe benefits, social security, and insurance of the joint ventures' Soviet employees. In general, the special legal norms regulate the relations connected with the establishment of joint ventures, the organization of their internal structure and management, taxation, and some other specific aspects of their activities affecting the interests of society and the state. Economic ties between joint ventures and other enterprises, associations, and organizations are normally covered by the general legislation.

The foregoing situation gives rise to the eminently sensible question: Is there a need for the existence of special legal norms for joint ventures operating on Soviet territory? Two considerations may be cited in support of such norms. First, under the conditions of the present-day structural and organizational forms of the functioning of the country's economy, such as the predominance of state enterprises and associations and cooperatives, a joint venture whose specifics would be determined by the participation of a foreign partner does not fit in with any kind of production body known to present Soviet legislation. Considering their internal structure—that is, the organization of the management of production with the participation of an administrative and work collective, and their outside connections with the higher-level state bodies and state planning in its present form—such production bodies are intended exclusively for Soviet citizens.

Second, the state provides for the interests of foreign investors by introducing special legal norms regulating joint ventures. This is particularly important in the earlier stages of the restructuring of the management of the Soviet economy, when the country does not yet have a stable market and many problems have to be solved with help from the state bodies.

The special legal norms regulating relations connected with the establishment and activities of joint ventures consequently will retain their importance in the future. Yet the future holds a gradual transition to the general rules for the legislative regulation of joint ventures, especially regarding their trade turnover. As wholesale trade in the country expands, as commodity and monetary relations develop, and as conditions are created for the introduction of the convertible ruble, there will no longer be any reason for special legal norms covering joint ventures. The legal norms regulating the internal structure of a joint venture and the norms of taxation will also be changed. The special legal regulations will retain their importance in the future for the determination of the procedure through which the participation of the foreign partner is secured, the shares of the Soviet and foreign partners in the authorized capital of a joint venture are valued, and in a number of other

issues based on the legislation on the legal regulation of a foreigner's status in the Soviet Union.

The transition to the general norms of the legal regulation of
joint ventures is already on. One example is the changed procedure for the operation of the supply system and the sale of the products of a joint venture. The old system, under which Soviet foreign
trade organizations posed as middlemen, as specified in Paragraph
26 of the Ruling of the Council of Ministers of September 17, 1987,
was replaced by the general system of contractual sales covering
state and cooperative enterprises. This process is greatly accelerated
at the present-day stage of legal reform development in the Soviet
Union. The legal foundations of the activities of joint ventures are
being strengthened. Article 28 of the Property Law as adopted by
the Supreme Soviet solves two essential issues concerning joint ventures: (1) transition to the legal form of joint entrepreneurship
used in all industrially developed countries of the world, and (2)
giving the subjects of joint entrepreneurship the property rights to
the facilities and equipment they have. According to Article 28 of
the law, "A joint venture with the participation of Soviet juridical
persons and foreign juridical persons is established on Soviet territory in the form of shareholding companies and other economic
societies and partnerships and may possess property required for
the conduct of the activities provided for by the constituent documents."

As was noted above, being prepared for consideration by the
Supreme Soviet, and soon to be adopted, is a Law on Shareholding
Companies and other kinds of economic partnerships that will
also cover joint ventures. To prevent production enterprises from
being slow to embrace market forms of economic life, a Provisional
Law on Shareholding Companies and Limited Liability
Companies passed by a Ruling of the Council of Ministers has been
put into effect. Unfortunately, the provisional law does not apply to
joint ventures.

There is no need to touch on the importance of giving the subjects of joint entrepreneurship the right of property to their facilities. This right would considerably expand the limits of their legal and economic freedom in every sphere of industrial, trade,
supply, and financial activities. To be sure, such a freedom cannot
be real unless the whole body of legislation regulating relations in

the field of property rights is brought into conformity with the emerging market situation in the Soviet Union. Such a task should be solved through the adoption of a second package of laws covered by the legal reform that is aimed at creating the necessary prerequisites for the functioning of a goods market, a capital market, and a labor market.

Article No. 28 of the Property Law contains another novel feature applicable to joint ventures—it expands the circle of the foreign participants in joint ventures in the Soviet Union, including foreign citizens as well as foreign juridical persons. At present, only foreign juridical persons can play such a role.

Finally, when dealing with the participation of foreign capital in entrepreneurship on Soviet territory, one cannot at present limit it to joint ventures. Such a position was correct before the adoption of the Property Law. But now, according to Article 30 of the law, foreign juridical bodies have the right to possess on Soviet territory industrial and other enterprises, buildings, structures, and other property for the purpose of economic and other kinds of activities, following the procedure laid down by the legislative acts of the Soviet Union and Union and autonomous republics. To provide for the realization of this right as laid down in Article 30, the Soviet Union and Union and autonomous republics are required to pass additional laws; nothing but these laws can lay the ground for the entrepreneurship of foreign juridical bodies on Soviet territory. It is probable that entrepreneurship of this kind may be stimulated in open economic zones. The Property Law also legalizes the property of foreign citizens and that of foreign countries and international organizations on Soviet territory.

Besides the general legal norms contained in individual laws adopted in the course of the radical economic reform, other laws continue to apply to joint ventures, including civil, labor, and other codes of laws, plus the normative acts issued on their basis dealing with supplies and capital construction. The Soviet Union is a country of codified legislation because, among other reasons, all individual laws, however important for the economy, should, in the final analysis, become part and parcel of the system of given legislation. After the adoption of such laws, all basic codifying normative acts will be drastically reconsidered. This can be described as the third stage of the legal reform under way in the Soviet Union.

In light of the foregoing, it would be natural to ask if it is necessary to have at present an individual normative act at the level of a
Law on Joint Ventures. It should also be noted that many existing
special legal norms covering joint ventures are dispersed among
various general normative acts. There is a difference of opinion on
this count. Some say this law is necessary and should contain the
norms laying down the particulars of the application of legislation
to the establishment and activities of joint ventures on Soviet territory.   Others disagree, saying that with every passing year, the
number of such particulars has shrunk. I believe that the latter
camp is right. All basic questions concerning joint ventures
should and can be solved on a common basis with the laws applied
to all other sectors of the Soviet economy under the conditions of a
regulated   market   economy.   The   issues   pertaining   to   the
citizenship or status of the participants in joint ventures and the
attendant questions can surely be solved in the general law and the
Law on the Status of Foreigners.

The provisions concerning joint ventures with the participation
of foreign capital on Soviet territory that have been discussed in
this paper are fully applicable to Soviet-U.S. joint ventures. Soviet
legislation makes no distinction between foreign companies investing in the Soviet economy, whatever their national identity.

11

Facilitating U.S.–Soviet
Joint Ventures through
Legislative Reform

Peter B. Maggs

INTRODUCTION

A more favorable legal climate could facilitate U.S.-Soviet joint ventures. Changes in the general legal system in the long run will be more important than adjustments of specific provisions of joint venture legislation. Since 1988, both the legislation on joint ventures and the legislation on the Soviet economy in which they operate have been unstable, unpredictable, and largely unpublished. Despite ambitious reform plans, Soviet legislation still falls far short of creating a workable operating environment for a domestic market economy. This fact has highly negative effects on the establishment and operation of joint ventures. In order to attract foreign capital at all, the Soviet government has had to give joint ventures more favorable legal treatment than domestic Soviet enterprises. However, this favored treatment has created a real danger of the emergence of "pseudo-joint-ventures," enterprises that are joint ventures in form but are really Soviet organizations seeking to escape government regulation. This danger in turn has lead to severe restrictions on the organization and operation of joint ventures. The fact that Soviet domestic prices reflect historical patterns rather than world market relationships created opportunities for joint ventures to import or produce goods that are overpriced in the Soviet Union and export goods that are underpriced. This imbalance has necessitated defensive legislation restricting exports by

joint ventures. However, this legislation closes one of the few
doors to profit remission by joint ventures.

AN END TO PREFERENTIAL TREATMENT
OF JOINT VENTURES

The Soviet Union is now promising to make major changes in the
substantive law regulating the Soviet economy, changes that could
eliminate the need for the current legal restrictions on joint ventures. On March 6, 1990, the Supreme Soviet adopted a Law on
Ownership. This legislation promised fundamental restructuring
of the law affecting both Soviet domestic enterprises and those with
foreign participation.[1] Nikolai Petrakov, a prominent adviser to
President Gorbachev, has indicated that there will be a speedup of
economic reform plans, with more rapid implementation of price
reforms and abolition of various ministries.[2] The Law on
Ownership could signal an end to the need for preferential treatment of joint ventures and an end as well to the various restrictions on their formation and operation. The Law on Ownership
provides, "joint enterprises with the participation of Soviet legal
persons and foreign legal persons and citizens are created on the
territory of the Soviet Union in the form of joint-stock companies,
business companies, and partnerships . . . ." These are the same
forms that the Law on Ownership creates for Soviet enterprises.
One may hope that the end result of the ongoing economic reforms will be the decent treatment of Soviet enterprises. In that
case, joint enterprises will not need special privileges. Then there
will be no reason for Soviet authorities to worry that Soviet organizations are setting up pseudo-joint-ventures, and it could become
possible to simplify the procedures for formation of joint ventures
by moving from a discretionary system, where bureaucrats decide
the terms under which a joint venture will be permitted, to a
declaratory system, under which the founders of a joint venture
merely need declare its existence to the authorities, who have no

---

1. "O Sobstvennosti v SSSR," *Izvestïya*, March 1, 1990, p. 2.
2. Interfax report, March 19, 1990.

power to object if the joint venture meets published legal requirements.

TRANSITION FROM A DISCRETIONARY TO A
DECLARATORY SYSTEM FOR CREATION OF ENTERPRISES

The fact that the Soviet system for the creation of enterprises is discretionary rather than declaratory is a major hindrance to the
creation of new joint ventures. I recently formed an American
corporation to engage in international trade business. I talked to
my lawyer for five minutes, and then to a legal secretary for about
ten minutes, giving details of the corporate structure I wanted. Two
weeks later, I received the corporate charter, stock certificates, and
my lawyer's bill. The bill, for US$185, covered all legal expenses
and all government filing fees. Those attempting to create joint
ventures face costs many times as great in terms of executive time,
legal fees, and uncertainties. The reason is the Soviet procedure,
which treats issuance of a corporate charter as a privilege rather
than as a right. Approval of a joint venture charter in the Soviet
Union appears to depend upon a combination of written rules, unwritten rules, official discretion, and support of persons in influential positions.

This initial barrier in cost and uncertainty serves as a much
greater barrier to small innovative enterprises than to large traditional enterprises. The small innovative enterprise enters into
risky ventures, where international competitive conditions make
time of the essence—if its product is a few months late getting to
market, the product is obsolete. (As former co-owner of a software
development business, I know the cruel world of capitalist competition all too well.) The Soviet procedures for joint venture formation greatly increase the "upfront" costs and hence the risks for
small businesses. It might not be unreasonable to count on initial
capital costs of US$100,000 in negotiating and legal expenses and
US$100,000 in the foreign share of the joint venture. (Soviet au-
thorities, contrary to the letter of the law, but perhaps relying on
secret unpublished regulations, appear to insist that the foreign
partner contribute substantial capital to a joint venture.) This is a
lot of money compared to the $185 I paid in the United States. The

most innovative joint ventures are highly risky. I have started about a dozen business ventures in the past ten or fifteen years. Most have been total failures, two have been extremely successful. However, because of the extraordinarily low capital costs of starting business ventures in the United States, I was able to go ahead, trying time and again until I had some success. I would never have started any of these ventures if I had been faced with the US$200,000 upfront cost of a Soviet joint venture. Since only one out of six of my business ventures succeeded, I would have had a prohibitively high capital cost of US$600,000 for each successful venture.

The result of this upfront cost has been an emphasis on larger Soviet-foreign joint ventures in areas other than those involving bringing speculative, high-technology products to market, in other words, in areas other than those where the Soviet economy most needs foreign expertise. In technical legal terms, the needed reform would appear to be fairly simple, namely, to provide for elimination of any minimum capital requirement and for issuance of a registration certificate to any applicant for a joint venture that met certain formal requirements. However, in fact, the reform is not that simple for two reasons: (1) the tendency of any bureaucracy to try to hold on to its power and keep operating in traditional patterns, and (2) the fact that, as mentioned above, Soviet law presently imposes intolerable burdens on all forms of enterprise other than joint ventures. As long as these burdens exist there will be pressure to create pseudo-joint-ventures, and there will be a perceived need to control the creation of joint ventures. Both the minimum capital requirement and the bureaucratic scrutiny can provide some control over the creation of such pseudo-joint-ventures.

FLEXIBILITY IN ORGANIZATIONAL STRUCTURE

The new Law on Ownership and the anticipated company law promise much greater flexibility in organizational structure for joint ventures. This should be a marked improvement on the current situation, which forces all joint ventures, large and small, into a single mode. It will also give flexibility to American companies in choosing a form that will have the most favorable treatment under U.S. tax law, which treats joint venture corporations more favorably in some circumstances and joint venture partnerships more favorably in other circumstances. The new legislation also opens the possibility of a very simple method of creating a joint venture: by a foreign firm's purchase of shares in a Soviet stock corporation.

AN END TO PRICE REGULATION

A key to creating a legal climate attractive for joint ventures is the end of government regulation of prices. While there are firm promises of price reform, to take place in 1990 and 1991, there has been no suggestion of abolition of the State Committee on Prices. The existence of price regulation causes pervasive legal difficulties for the establishment of joint ventures. It causes underpricing and thus forces the Soviet government to create export restrictions on joint ventures, such as those in the March 1989 Decree. It causes shortages, thus making it difficult for joint ventures to obtain necessary supplies and services, such as housing. Finally, no progress can be made toward a convertible ruble without the abolition of price regulation, since the distortions caused by price regulation prevent the ruble from functioning as a universal measure of value, that is, from performing the function of money.

ANTIMONOPOLY LEGISLATION

The existence of numerous monopolies in the Soviet economy is a barrier to freeing prices to seek market levels, because these monopolies would then charge exploitative monopoly prices. The problem is compounded by the fact that not only does the Soviet Union lack antimonopoly legislation, it in fact has legislation guaranteeing various organizations monopolies, particularly in such important service areas as communications, banking, and transportation. To date, the solution to the monopoly problem has been found in price regulation. However, this solution creates many problems for joint ventures. Often, services (for example, telephone services) are very difficult to obtain because demand greatly exceeds supply at the regulated prices. Monopoly enterprises, unable to obtain profits by high prices, instead exploit their monopolies by offering poorer and poorer service for the same fixed prices. The contrast between areas of the Soviet economy where competition is legally allowed or at least tolerated and those where competition is still nonexistent or forbidden is extraordinary. The toleration of licensed and unlicensed private taxicabs in Moscow creates a competitive market in which foreign entrepreneurs can get to their business appointments as easily and quickly as in other major world capitals. On the other hand, a simple banking transaction can take 1,000 times longer than the same transaction in a foreign country.

PROTECTION OF PROPERTY RIGHTS

Although the new Law on Ownership promises considerably improved protection of property rights, a number of gaps remain in Soviet property right protection. The anticipated conclusion of a U.S.-Soviet investment protection treaty will buttress the guarantees of the ownership law. Difficulties remain in the areas of intellectual property and land title.

Soviet intellectual property law antedates the joint venture era and is clearly inadequate for protecting the interests of the very type of high-technology joint venture that the Soviet Union should be attracting. The Soviet government in 1989 published a draft patent law and hinted that it would adhere to the Berne Copyright Convention. However, the patent law remains stalled in the legislative logjam caused by the attempt to push a huge mass of perestroika legislation through the new more democratic (and hence slower) lawmaking process. The increasing shortage of hard currency has stalled Berne Convention ratification, because obligations under that Convention would require the Soviet Union to pay for some rights it now takes gratis. A member of the committee drafting Soviet software protection legislation has shared drafts with and has been responsive to suggestions from American specialists, including the author of this paper, in computer program copyright. This cooperation has produced excellent draft legislation, but progress toward enactment has been glacial. Soviet law remains very unclear on employee rights in inventions and on trade secrets.

Land title law has never been important in the Soviet Union because not only the land but all major structures have belonged to the government. The new Fundamentals of Land Legislation continue the principle of government ownership of land. Joint ventures can, however, obtain land as part of the Soviet partners' contribution or by leasing. However, it is proving very difficult for foreign investors to be certain that those claiming to be able to provide land have, in fact, the right to do so. There is no government program of land title guarantee, and there are no land title insurance companies in the Soviet Union. If the Soviet Union wants foreign companies to invest millions of dollars in structures on Soviet soil, it must find some way to guarantee to them that they have the necessary land rights.

NEWLY EMERGING LEGAL PROBLEMS

In some ways, the legal backwardness of the Soviet Union has made the opening of joint ventures easier. As compared to many other countries, the Soviet Union has much weaker legislative and bureaucratic regulations on such matters as environmental protection, occupational health and safety, consumer product safety, product liability, regulation of advertising, protection of the rights of women and minorities, and the rights of trade unions. Over the coming years, the Soviet Union is likely to increase the level of legal regulations in these areas at the same time it is decreasing legal regulation in other areas. While one can only applaud improvements in environmental protection, safety, and individual rights, one must realize that each new area of government regulation imposes legal burdens on business ventures. Even if price and planning controls wither away, there will be a real need, if joint ventures are to succeed, for there to be a legal culture that allows enterprises to know their rights and obligations and get good legal advice and representation.

TREATIES

Recent statements by Soviet and U.S. officials have indicated that three significant treaty developments will soon occur. These are the negotiation of a new tax treaty, the negotiation of an investment guarantee treaty, and the admission of the Soviet Union to observer status in the General Agreement on Tariffs and Trade (GATT). In addition, the United States and the Soviet Union are expected to grant one another most favored nation status for imports.

The new tax treaty will reduce legal overhead costs for joint ventures. The existing U.S.-Soviet tax treaty was signed before it was possible for American businesses to invest in Soviet enterprises. As a result, it contained no provision exempting remittance of dividends from taxation. The result was not really additional tax, but additional legal and organizational expenses. American companies have been able to avoid the tax by creating subsidiaries in countries whose tax treaties with the Soviet Union have provisions exempting remittances from taxation. This has been possible because for some reason Soviet authorities have failed to follow the international custom of insisting upon an "anti-tax-shopping" provision in Soviet tax treaties. But, in order to avoid taxes, American companies have had considerable extra expenses because they must hire local lawyers and pay local incorporation fees in the countries where they create the subsidiaries. American partners in small joint ventures are in a worse position—they must pay the tax because they cannot afford the high cost of creating a foreign subsidiary. The new U.S.-Soviet tax treaty should contain a provision exempting dividend remissions from taxation.

The new Soviet income tax legislation establishes much higher top rates of tax on income. Therefore, it will be important in facilitating joint ventures for the new tax treaty to provide American managers and technicians working for joint ventures exemption from high Soviet taxes. To attract qualified personnel to work abroad, American companies must guarantee to pay enough additional salary to cover any additional taxes incurred by working abroad. Without appropriate exemptions under the tax treaty, Americans could be subject to Soviet taxes, and so their companies would have to pay them very substantial additional amounts (to cover not only the Soviet taxes, but in some cases the U.S. taxes on the additional compensation). These high costs would discourage American companies from creating joint ventures and from sending qualified personnel to transfer know-how to joint ventures.

An investment guarantee treaty providing assurances against the risk of expropriation could provide some further assurance to potential foreign investors. However, it is unlikely that such a treaty would have a significant effect on the volume of investment because it appears that fear of expropriation ranks very low among the worries of potential American joint venture partners.

In the long run, if a market economy emerges in the Soviet Union, one can hope that it will advance to full GATT membership, and that it and the United States will dismantle the many trade barriers that exist between the two countries. The admission of the Soviet Union to observer status in the GATT and the granting by the United States of most favored nation status are important steps in this direction.

LEGAL CULTURE

The creation of Soviet joint ventures is discouraged by the relative underdevelopment of certain aspects of the legal climate in the Soviet Union. There are almost no private law firms experienced in giving advice on international business law. Administrative rulemaking proceeds with little opportunity for input from interested parties. Key administrative regulations are unpublished. Judicial review of administrative action remains underdeveloped, despite recent progress. There are no commercial courts and no arbitration body that draw on arbitrators from an international pool of specialists. These factors combine to create high information costs and a perception of high "legal risks" and thus discourage joint ventures. As joint ventures move from a special position into the mainstream of the Soviet economy, these problems will intensify. Foreign lawyers and a few Soviet law firms have provided expertise on the narrow area of joint venture law; continued foreign pressure has caused the publication or "leaking" of the most important administrative regulations affecting joint ventures. The situation both with respect to the availability of legal expertise and the publication of regulations is much worse with respect to the general Soviet economy.

Law Firms

The Soviet Union has been among the most liberal countries in the world in toleration of law practice by unlicensed lawyers from foreign countries, but it has been one of the most backward in the development of legal expertise of its own for giving advice to foreign firms. American and British law firms have received excellent cooperation from Soviet authorities in opening offices in Moscow, in sharp contrast to the severe resistance that foreign lawyers have faced in Tokyo and other world capitals. However, there is a severe shortage of Americans with a knowledge of the Soviet legal system and experience in conducting transactions in the Soviet Union. A number of those who are so qualified are unwilling to move to Moscow because of their family situation or other personal reasons. Hourly charges of American lawyers are very high; they become even higher at the premium rates charged by the foreign branches of American law firms. Foreign law firm offices have been concentrated in Moscow. A business executive conducting negotiations in Siberia or Armenia, for example, will not find any U.S. legal advisers familiar with local officialdom.

The limited availability, limited expertise, and high cost of American lawyers mean that foreign firms strongly need the assistance of Soviet law firms in the organization and operation of joint ventures. Here there have been and are problems, but solutions seem to be emerging. Practicing Soviet lawyers have lacked independence and experience in international business law and have been more oriented toward litigation than transaction planning. Soviet law seems to be tolerating the creation of private law firms specializing in giving advice on international business transactions. These firms at first took the form of cooperatives, and then the form of joint ventures after restrictive legislation and popular resentment made the cooperative form less attractive. One may hope that law firms may in the future use the variety of organizational forms offered by the new Law on Ownership and the promised company law.

The emergence of experienced and competitive law firms in major Soviet cities capable of providing expert legal advice to potential foreign partners in joint ventures will be of great value in encouraging and shaping these transactions. This is particularly true because it may be much easier to develop a cadre of Soviet lawyers experienced in dealing with the Soviet bureaucracy than to reform or eliminate that bureaucracy.

Administrative Rulemaking

Soviet administrative rulemaking procedures cause great difficulties for joint ventures. Rarely do Soviet administrative agencies give parties to be affected a chance to be heard before a new rule is adopted. A huge portion of Soviet administrative regulations are unpublished and inaccessible. At present, joint ventures are somewhat insulated from the Soviet economy. This means that the most important rules affecting joint ventures come from only two organizations, the Ministry of Finance and the State Committee on Foreign Economic Relations. At least some of the officials of these organizations have been cooperative in releasing regulations and in predicting changes in regulations for joint ventures. However, as economic restructuring brings joint ventures more into the mainstream of the Soviet economy, they will be subject to regulation by a large number of government agencies. They will face the same problems of unpredictability and inaccessibility of administrative regulations that so many Soviet enterprises now complain about.

Judicial Review

There are no adequate channels for judicial review of administrative regulations and decisions of administrative agencies. Recent Soviet legislation has broadened powers of judicial review of administrative decisions affecting citizens and has granted enterprises the power to sue "superior agencies." The former right is of no use to companies. The later right has existed more on paper than in practice. It will become meaningless when "superior

agencies" are transformed into regulatory bodies with the implementation of the promised elimination of ministerial hierar-
chies. The new Commission on Constitutional Review lacks the
power to consider the legality of administrative agency decisions.

Dispute Resolution

The Soviet Union lacks adequate mechanisms for the resolution of
commercial disputes. This lack could create serious problems if
joint ventures find themselves operating directly in the Soviet domestic economy, with contract and other legal relations with large
numbers of other Soviet enterprises. This particularly will be true
if the Darwinistic philosophy of the more radical Soviet reformers
becomes law, and enterprises are subjected to a regime of "survival
of the fittest." There are no commercial courts, and the regular
judges are inexperienced in commercial matters. The personnel
of State Arbitration does have considerable experience in commercial matters, but only in the implementation of the outmoded
"command-administrative" system. The only available arbitration
tribunal, the Arbitration Court of the Soviet Chamber of Commerce
and Industry, is highly parochial, in that all members of its arbitration panels are Soviet citizens. Furthermore, if a joint venture
takes the form of an ordinary Soviet joint-stock corporation, the
Arbitration Court may have no legal basis for jurisdiction over disputes between the joint venture and another Soviet corporation.

CONCLUSION

The new phase of perestroika promises to move joint ventures from
the periphery to the center of Soviet economic life. This move will
make the success of joint ventures depend much more upon the
general quality of the Soviet system of legal regulation of economic
activity. At present, this system falls far short of providing the
minimum legal guarantees necessary for the proper operation of a
market economy. If the Soviet Union succeeds in developing a

modern system of commercial law, there will be some benefit to joint ventures, but by far the greatest benefit will be to the Soviet economy as a whole.

12

Can Joint Ventures Help
to Create a Market Economy
in the Soviet Union?

Alexander L. Katkov

THE CRISIS IN THE SOVIET ECONOMY

There is no question that the Soviet economy requires radical change in all aspects. These changes should include the design and implementation of a new economic mechanism based on a new approach to using such basic economic categories as ownership and property, market and competition, foreign collaboration, and foreign investment.

Over the past decades, directive planning and state ownership led to the creation of an administrative and highly centralized system of management and to the decrease of individual motivation of producers to undertake effective work and to engage in risk-taking entrepreneurship. The results were the stagnation of economic development, decreasing growth rates of output and productivity, the expansion of the capital stock without corresponding increases in productivity and in the technological level of output, growing imbalances in the national economy itself, and, as final results, the growing deficit in the state budget, increasing disequilibration of the consumer market, the overhang of unwanted personal savings, and the growth of inflation. A contradiction between two needs, the need to increase the Soviet internal market's output of consumer goods and the need for the modernization of the industrial and agricultural sectors' productive capacities, poses a very complicated dilemma for the management of the investment process.

Many economists and business leaders in the Soviet Union now are beginning to understand that the reform of ownership relations and the financial mechanism are the central points of the economic reform in general. The weak, inconvertible ruble is a key barrier to the movement toward a market economy. To create real economic relations between Soviet producers of commodities and services and their customers both inside and outside the country, real, instead of artificial, market and commodity-money relationships should be organized.

The separation of the producer from the means of production and from the economic consequences of its efforts are consequences of the state monopoly over means of production; the monopoly of producers that supports the artificial pricing system and leads to supply delays and low quality; overcentralized management resulting in a lack of personal responsibility for decisionmaking, low managerial qualifications; the building up of administrative barriers to initiative and entrepreneurship; and the paralysis of the credit and financial system. All these factors are blocking the movement of the Soviet economy toward a single national market and are hampering efforts to develop a coherent economic policy to fight the current economic crisis.

This situation is aggravated by the contradictions and differences between a consumer's ruble as a means of payment and an enterprise ruble, which does not serve a similar role in the market for industrial inputs. Thus, the consumer market in the Soviet Union is separated from the market of means of production. Everything can be sold for cash on the consumer market. But industrial inputs, machinery, and equipment can be bought by an enterprise only if it has a fund—that is, permission of the authorities to buy this commodity. Rubles used in transactions for funded inputs are called allocated rubles, and they differ in their role as a medium of payment from the consumer rubles. For purchases of specific equipment, the allocated ruble is more valuable, but outside the scope of this concrete transaction authorized by the firm's superiors, this ruble is little more than a piece of paper. The unification of these two financial markets and the creation of a single ruble that can serve as a medium of payment equally for consumer and producer goods is one of the immediate tasks in creating a single, national integrated market.

Some figures discussed during December 1989 by the Second Congress of People's Deputies and the Supreme Soviet show that the Soviet economy is now in a critical situation. The instability of the national finance system produced a huge deficit in the state budget. While the state's income remained relatively fixed from 1985 to 1989, budgetary expenditures grew rapidly. As a result, the deficit in the state budget grew from 18 billion rubles in 1985 to 120 billion rubles in 1989. The inflationary effects are exacerbated by the serious supply shortages, which, for many consumer goods and services, have jumped to close 10 percent per year. As a result, consumers are forced to hold 300 billion rubles worth of deposits in saving banks, and no less money is frozen in home savings. The growth of money emission accompanied the budgetary deficit, which increased from 4 billion rubles in 1985 to 34 billion rubles in 1989. The annual growth of money incomes of the Soviet population during 1989 was 9 percent, or twice as high as planned; at the same time, the growth of commodity turnover reached only 6 percent.

As purchasing power grew faster than supply, hidden growth of prices resulted, which also stimulated the further growth of the commodity and service markets' deficits. The unfavorable conditions of the world trade situation in the past several years, the long-term orientation of the national economy toward the export of raw materials and fuels, and the import of equipment and food led to the growth of the external debt to US$55 billion. By 1988, the Soviet Union lost US$23.4 billion as a result of declining world oil prices and increases in world market prices of food and equipment. All of these losses are the consequence of the economy's outmoded structure of production and of managerial mistakes made in the distant and not so distant past.

SOLVING THE CRISIS: THE NEED FOR RADICAL ECONOMIC REFORM

To solve these problems, the government has designed a program for reconstructing the national economy step by step. Components of the program, adopted in December 1989 by the Soviet Parliament, include:

146 THE EMERGING RUSSIAN BEAR

1. development of a new legal system for economic relations that will support the structural changes envisioned in the national economy;
2. reduction of state expenditures, including the reduction of centralized capital investments in industry, military spending, and expenditures for maintenance of the state management apparatus;
3. reallocation of investment to increase the volume of consumer commodities' production;
4. improvement of the credit and tax system; and
5. reduction of money emission and control of wage growth.

The emergency nature of the economic situation will shorten the time available for the transition to the new system. The economy needs radical and rapid changes to move it toward a market mechanism. What kind of economic changes can be discussed as appropriate for the current situation? Can some economic structures that now exist in the Soviet economy be used as the nucleus of the new economic mechanism?

From our point of view, the acceleration of the transformation to a market mechanism will be possible only if the transformation of the property relationships and the construction of the new national market are realized with the deeper and wider integration of the Soviet economy into the world economy, thus implying the adoption of all economic, financial, and managerial tools used by the world economic society. The most important elements that need to be imported into the reformed Soviet economic system are outlined below.

Creation of Multiownership Forms of Enterprises

As indicated in the plan for economic reform submitted to the Soviet Parliament by Mikhail Gorbachev soon after his nomination to president, the previous government plan for step-by-step economic changes will be replaced by a more radical plan that will include emergency economic changes. Such a plan should include as its basic points changes in ownership relations and financial and investment policy.

When we speak about moving from central planning and state ownership to free-market and multiproprietary forms of ownership, the key issue becomes the privatization of state-owned enterprises. There are some models of the privatization of state-owned enterprises that have been put forward by economists and politicians from both the East and West. *Business Week* magazine, in its February 5, 1990, issue, summarized the them into five main models:

1. the Sell-Off Model;
2. the Cross-Ownership Model;
3. the ESOP (Employee Stock-Ownership Plan) Model;
4. the Social Dividend Model; and
5. the Entrepreneurial Model.

Each of these models has advantages and drawbacks, but some common factors can be found that transform them into a sort of a sick economy's treatment. To find those common traits we should first pick out the main symptoms of the economic disease: the lack of managerial and entrepreneurial freedom and limitations to competition. The restrictions on the possibility of pursuing capital spending programs, modernization and restructuring of the manufacturing processes, and the hiring and firing of personnel block most incentives and innovations. As a result, there is a slowdown in responses to changes in the world economic process. The consequences of this lack of adaptation are a permanent lag in adaptation to changes in the world economic environment, an accelerating backwardness in industrial structure, and low growth rates of output and productivity.

Looking at the privatization models, it is evident that—except for the Sell-Off Model, which is based on selling state-owned enterprises to incumbent management or foreign companies—they propose to restructure the economy by converting state-owned companies into shareholding companies or corporations. The differences among them are connected with the definitions of shareholder status and managerial structure. For example, the ESOP model proposes to convert companies or divisions into worker-owned firms where each employee makes a small outlay but banks and government provide most of the financing required to enable the workers to purchase the shares. The Social-Dividend Model proposes to convert state companies into corporations with marketable shares, so that each citizen gets a portfolio of stocks as a sort of social dividend. The Cross-Ownership Model suggests formation of a new set of parent companies consisting of closely linked networks of suppliers and creditors where key units own stakes in each other. The Entrepreneurial Model tries to find a compromise between the ESOP and the Sell-Off models, proposing the creation of new forms of partnerships, cooperatives, and small private firms to encourage managers and workers at large companies to start new ventures in-house without buying the large company itself.

The common idea of all these approaches is an attempt to design a flexible economic structure that simultaneously gives workers and managers opportunities to participate in the management and distribution of the enterprise's profit, protects the enterprise from being pushed and pulled by state agencies, and opens the door for the fresh wind of incentives, inventions, and investments. Moreover, these new enterprises are not protected from the possibility of failure and bankruptcy.

The purchase of state-owned enterprises by workers will motivate them to work hard and efficiently and will create pressures for a more efficient management. Shareholding companies will not only pay incomes to their workers that reflect the results of enterprise operations, they will also guarantee the pensions, social insurance, and medical service to these workers. Although the idea is not very new, it is not obvious how to implement it, especially taking into consideration a number of large and small problems that will face any Soviet reformer.

To economic problems discussed earlier, we should add the political instability based not only on economic problems but also on growth of national and ethnic conflicts and social differences inside the society. But the threshold is under our feet, and, whether we move forward or back, the uncertainty is very high. The main difference is in our knowledge of the outcomes. If we move back, we know, from past experience, the consequences. In moving forward, we have only a preliminary forecast obtained by extrapolating the as yet incomplete experience of other countries such as Poland and Hungary.

To support a policy of moving forward we should not only design and build up new structures and mechanisms, we should also make maximum use of already existing structures and mechanisms.

JOINT VENTURES IN THE SOVIET UNION

From our point of view, one of the most important elements of the current Soviet economy is the joint venture. The joint venture (JV) is a partnership with a limited liability or a limited liability company. It can operate in most aspects independently of the central planning authorities and even from state-owned parents who are the Soviet participants in a JV.

The positive features of JVs are that they:

1. are organized as multi-ownership entities;
2. have new capital, technology, and foreign expertise in the key areas of management, quality control, and marketing;
3. operate as business ventures and therefore are more oriented toward innovation and the use of incentives; and
4. use a policy of social dividends to motivate the staff and workers to work efficiently.

Nevertheless, there are also some negative elements that characterize JVs, namely, they:

1. currently make up a too small part of the Soviet economy;
2. represent an insufficient amount of foreign investment and a narrow spectrum of modern technology;
3. have encountered some difficulties and restrictions as a result of ruble inconvertibility and the absence of an organized domestic market.

Going back to the privatization road map analyzed in *Business Week*, we can see that it is possible to use JVs as a key element in designing a new Soviet economy that will be market-oriented and deeply involved in the global economy. Before analyzing a transition from JVs to shareholding companies, we look at the history of the process of establishing JVs in the Soviet Union for a better understanding of some fundamental tendencies.

THE SOVIET UNION AND THE WORLD ECONOMY

The Soviet Union's growing integration into the world economy and more active participation in the international division of labor were the main reasons for the fundamental restructuring of the foreign trade system. The restructuring began in 1986, and among its objectives were the more rapid growth of the volume of foreign trade and qualitative changes in the structure of Soviet exports and imports in the management of foreign economic relations, and in the wider use of progressive forms of cooperation.

The Soviet Union's annual foreign trade turnover reached its peak of 140 billion rubles in 1985, thanks in large part to high world oil prices. In subsequent years, the total volume declined, in large part due to decreases in energy and raw material prices (Table 12-1).

More than 140 countries are now among the Soviet Union's trading partners, but the Soviet Union's share in world trade, 4-5 percent, does not correspond to the country's potential. The general picture of the Soviet Union's trade with leading western countries is presented in Table 12-2.

To change this situation, the Soviet Union seeks to increase exports of finished products and manufactured goods, especially of engineering products, including the most sophisticated and technology-intensive ones. Also, the Soviet Union began to adopt new and more progressive forms of cooperation, including cooperation in production and in science and technology, the establishment of direct economic ties, and the establishment of JVs and international associations. Some locations in the Soviet Union (for example, Leningrad, Nakhodka, and Vyborg) are now being declared by the Russian Parliament as future zones of joint entrepreneurship or free-trade zones.

Additional concrete steps have been taken to improve the foreign economic activity of the Soviet Union during the last three years. In January 1987, a number of Soviet sectors and enterprises were granted the right to enter the world market and undertake

Table 12-1. Soviet Foreign Trade
(Billions of Rubles)

	1950	1960	1970	1980	1985	1987	1988	1989
Exports	1.6	5.0	11.5	49.6	72.7	68.2	67.1	68.2
Imports	1.3	5.1	10.6	44.5	69.4	60.7	65.0	70.2
Total Turnover	2.9	10.1	22.1	94.1	142.1	128.9	132.1	138.4

Sources: Vladimir Kamentsev, *Economic Ties, A Prerequisite of Lasting Peace* (Moscow: Novosti Press Agency Publishing House, 1988); *Moscow International Business*, no. 1, 1990, p. 15.

Table 12-2. Soviet Trade with Leading Western Countries in 1987 and 1988
(Million Rubles)

Country	Trade Turnover		Exports		Imports	
	1987	1988	1987	1988	1987	1988
Austria	1031	1167	431	455	600	712
Belgium	1105	1147	738	771	366	376
Canada	497	551	47	16	450	535
FRG	4957	5629	2327	2397	2630	3231
Finland	3743	3717	1707	1528	2036	2188
France	2608	2769	1518	1579	1090	1190
Italy	3491	3034	1804	1691	1687	1343
Japan	2601	3135	973	1184	1628	1952
Netherlands	1013	934	781	657	232	278
Sweden	652	707	427	467	225	246
United Kingdom	2111	2417	1586	1794	524	623
USA	1198	2104	279	331	919	1773

Source: Kamentsev *(op. cit.)*

export and import operations without the intermediation of the Soviet Ministry of Foreign Trade and the other few government bodies that exercise a monopoly over foreign trade. In 1987, this right was accorded to 23 ministries and 80 leading associations and enterprises. In April 1989, this right was extended to all Soviet associations, enterprises, and cooperatives that produced a product competitive on the international market.

The other important step was the formation in January 1988 of the Ministry of Foreign Economic Relations. The Ministry of Foreign Trade and the State Committee for Foreign Economic Relations were abolished.

A third step was the organization of the State Foreign Economic Commission, which coordinates the work of all ministries and departments engaged in foreign economic activity, the Ministry of Foreign Economic Relations, the Bank for Foreign Economic Activity, the State Customs House, and sectoral ministries. The main task of the Commission is to create the optimum conditions for the work of all those who are connected with the world market and give them direction and guidelines.

The fourth step was granting the right to undertake export and import operations to each enterprise, leading association, and co-operative that produce products or services that have the potential to export. This right was declared by a Decree of the Soviet Council of Ministers in December 1988.

Ensuring the observance of state interests on the foreign market is the duty of the Ministry of Foreign Economic Relations. Two Decrees of the Soviet Council of Ministers from March and December 1989 obliged all participants in external economic relations to be registered by the Ministry of Foreign Economic Relations and also required them to obtain a license to export and import. In some respects, the decrees seek to regulate the new, decentralized system of foreign trade in the old traditions of the state monopoly on foreign trade, and therefore this step can be viewed as a step back. However, there are some objective reasons for the measures because of the dangers of drastic disorganization of the domestic commodity market. Under the new system, all exporters would begin to search the possibility of selling something abroad in order to earn hard currency. Domestic consumers thus would face shortages as goods were indiscriminately directed for export.

Also, the Ministry of Foreign Economic Relations continues to handle a number of operations, including export and import of fuels, raw materials, food and other products of national importance, and the construction and commissioning of various projects being built with Soviet assistance abroad.

Until the restructuring of the Soviet Union's foreign economic relations system, the foreign trade activity of Soviet enterprises was valued in domestic wholesale prices, which differed significantly from world prices. Now, an enterprise's performance is evaluated in actual contract prices, which are converted into rubles by means of special coefficients, assuring a uniform cost-accounting system for an enterprise's external and internal operations. A radical reform of the price system will be carried out at the beginning of the next five-year plan period. In particular, the ratios of domestic prices for certain groups of products will be brought into conformity with world prices during the course of the reform. In the future, foreign currency exchange rates will be used as the Soviet economy gradually ensures the convertibility of the ruble.

CHARACTERISTICS OF JVs IN THE SOVIET UNION

The main laws and decrees regulating JV operations in the Soviet Union are Decree of the Presidium of the USSR Supreme Soviet on Questions Concerning the Establishment on the Territory of the USSR and Operation of Joint Ventures, International Amalgamations and Organizations with the Participation of Soviet and Foreign Organizations, Firms and Management Bodies of January 13, 1987, and Decree No. 49, Decree of the USSR Council of Ministers on the Establishment on the Territory of the USSR and Operation of Joint Ventures with the Participation of Soviet Organizations and Firms from Capitalist and Developing Countries of January 13, 1987. A JV can be established in the industry and service sectors of the economy. There are no limitations on the number of partners, the size of a JV's capital, or the foreign partner's share of the capital.

As Table 12-3 shows, more than 1,500 JVs have been registered by the Ministry of Finance, though only some of them have begun to operate and generate profits. However, the number of registered

JVs is growing rapidly, indicating the strong desire of foreign firms to establish a presence in the Soviet market in the form of a JV, because direct foreign investment in the Soviet is as yet impossible. The information in tables 12-4 and 12-5, which reflects the situation with joint entrepreneurship in the Soviet Union in June and October 1989, can help to illustrate the main trends of development of this process. Even if the total number of ventures has approximately tripled since the data were compiled, the main proportions have not changed very much.

During 1989, the government of the Soviet Union made active efforts to create Zones of Joint Entrepreneurship. These zones will be experimental entities that are planned to be centers of new technological and managerial experiments. They should work first to supply the Soviet domestic market and to develop the economies of the regions where zones will be situated. Taxation and customs regimes are planned to be attractive for foreign investors, who can be not only partners in JVs established in these zones, but can also organize their own companies, affiliates, and subsidiaries with 100 percent foreign ownership. A large share of the goods produced in the zones can be exported abroad. Zones will be organized not only near the national border of the Soviet Union but on the territories of regions situated inside the country. More than 20 regions of the Soviet Union wish to establish on their territory Zones of Joint Entrepreneurship. Two projects, Nakhodka and Vyborg, will be ready in 1990.

The Law on Zones of Joint Entrepreneurship is now at the drafting stage, and thus it is difficult to discuss the main principles of the zones' status and conditions for economic activity. Nevertheless, some details of the basic approach can be outlined, and there are some basic problems that must be decided by this law:

1. All kinds of ownership should be allowed on the zone's territory, and each should have the equivalent right for the development.
2. Zones should have a sound monetary and credit system based on hard currency, and therefore on the territory of these zones; a convertible gold ruble should be put into operation;
3. Using world market prices, a special system of privileges and preferences should be designed for enterprises operating on a

Table 12-3. Number of Joint Ventures Registered

Year	Month J	F	M	A	M	J	J	A	S	O	N	D	Total
1987	-	-	-	-	1	4	2	-	1	3	3	9	23
1988	6	-	7	5	10	12	9	16	17	8	30	48	168
1989	41	46	87	53	102			413 (J-O)			341 (O-D)		1083

Table 12-4. Joint Ventures by Types of Owner
(June, October 1989)

Foreign Partner's Type of Country	Number J[b]	Number O[c]	% J	% O	Statute Capital[a] J	Statute Capital[a] O	% J	% O
With Partners from Soc. Countries	59	105	11.3	11.3	244.6	352.1	15.0	14.1
With Partners from Cap. Countries	414	748	79.6	80.2	1309.9	2036.2	80.2	81.3
With Partners from Dev. Countries	34	60	6.5	6.4	44.8	63.2	2.7	2.5
With Partners from Cap. and Dev. Countries (Mix)	6	8	1.2	0.8	24.8	27.9	1.5	1.1
With Partners from Soc. and Cap. Countries (Mix)	7	12	1.4	1.3	9.1	26.2	0.6	1.0
With Partners from Soc. and Dev. Countries (Mix)	0	0	0	0	0	0	0	0
Total	520	933	100.0		1633.2	2505.6	100.0	

a. Millions of rubles.
b. J = June.
c. O = October.

zone's territory to stimulate the development of products reflecting national priorities.

It is understandable that the regulatory framework for each zone can vary depending on the type of zone, the goal of its development, available resources, and even on the zone's location. For example, Nakhodka as a gateway between the Pacific hemisphere and Siberia will be, from its first steps, oriented toward the maximum utilization of natural resources located east of the Urals. Such locational advantages—with railroads, air and water transportation of cargo, a good climate, agricultural facilities, and accessibility to a multitude of natural resources—can be seen as factors stimulating foreign investors toward this region. Compared to Nakhodka as a the new door to the East, the Leningrad and Vyborg zones look like the old window to the West (Vyborg is 90 miles north of Leningrad). The Leningrad and Vyborg zones offer no great possibilities for the utilization of Soviet natural resources, but they can lean on the intellectual and cultural resources and traditions of the European part of the Soviet Union, especially Leningrad, with its high intellectual and industrial potential and historical and cultural significance and attractiveness.

It is very important that Zones of Joint Entrepreneurship be considered not only as sources of currency and new technologies and skills, but as experimental laboratories for finding workable mechanisms for transforming central planning to a market economy.

A new custom tariff for the Soviet Union will be prepared for introduction in 1991. This tariff will regulate not only the customs regime on the territory of the enterprise zones, but it will also regulate the competition between domestic and imported goods, thus helping to reform prices. The Soviet importer will pay duties and include them into the cost of his own production. Therefore, the importer will compare the costs of buying goods on the domestic and world markets. The state will have the right of operative nontariff regulation of foreign operations—by quotas on export and import, for example—because demands of the Soviet domestic market in some kinds of goods and the imbalance of payment in some sectors of foreign trade require it. Joint ventures are free from quotas and licenses in export operations of their own production and in import operations for their own industrial and social needs.

Table 12-5. Joint Ventures by Branch of Industry

Branch of Industry Type of Country	Number		%	
	June	Oct.	June	Oct.
Fuel and Energy	3	5	0.6	0.5
Metallurgy	2	5	0.4	0.5
Chemicals and Forestry	30	47	5.7	5.0
Machine Building	28	40	5.4	4.3
Computers and Software	64	122	12.3	13.1
Construction and Constr. Materials	19	60	3.6	6.4
Transport and Communications	8	18	1.5	1.9
Agriculture	30	41	5.7	4.4
Services in R&D, Engineering Training and Consultancy	156	287	30.0	30.8
Social Needs Sector (Total)	172	308	33.1	40.7
Retail and Food Services	34	58	6.5	6.2
Tourism and Hotel Services	26	53	5.0	5.7
Medicine and Health Services	29	46	5.6	4.9
Consumer Goods	46	58	8.9	6.2
Printing and Publishing	13	25	2.5	2.7
Cinema, Video Production, Concerts	24	37	4.6	4.0
Others	8	31	1.5	3.3
Total	520	933	100.0	100.0

All these steps on the way to restructuring the foreign economic relations system will help to stabilize the Soviet ruble inside the country. Together with the price reform and the reform of wholesale trade, they will help to create conditions for the ruble's convertibility. It is clear that the success of perestroika in many aspects depends on positive changes in the integration of the Soviet Union into the world economy. Thus, the Soviet economy is now being opened to suggestions for industrial collaboration.

The previous analysis suggests that the growth of the number of JVs established in the Soviet Union and the growth of foreign investment reflect an intensified interest in investing in the Soviet Union. The concern of foreign investors about the lack of guarantees for their investments and the repatriation of profits in hard currency is one of the main reasons for the small number of fully operating JVs. Moreover, many restrictions, which are the result of contradictions between market-oriented JVs and the centralized planning economic environment, limit the positive effects of JVs on the rest of the Soviet economy.

To make JVs a more active transition element on the way to a market economy, three things are required:

1. The new law on joint-stock companies in the Soviet Union, including basic regulations about establishing central and regional stock exchanges, should be adopted by the Soviet Parliament as soon as possible.
2. The new law on external economic relations, which will include all regulations for JVs, should not contradict the law about joint-stock companies and eliminate most restrictions on foreign investors and the difference in rights between Soviet and foreign investors.
3. All restrictions on foreign trade with the Soviet Union enacted in the past by foreign governments should be eliminated.

Design of New Possibilities for Foreign Investments

There is a common opinion now that the foremost difficulty in establishing an efficient operation of JVs in the Soviet Union and organizing any other form of investment initiative is the inconvertibility of the Soviet ruble, which creates obstacles to the repatriation profit from investments. The creation of convertibility on the basis of auctions, as discussed at the Geonomics seminar in October 1989, is too slow a way in the current critical situation. A quicker way probably lies in the elimination of all barriers to foreign investments and the approval of 100 percent foreign ownership of Soviet companies in some sectors of industry and in services. The Polish and Hungarian experiences show us that this can produce positive results. It is very significant that in Hungary both laws connected with structural reform and foreign investment were adopted at the same time and were interrelated. The Hungarian Companies Act and the Foreign Investment Act of January 1989 provide a foundation for Hungarian citizens and corporate entities to establish shareholding companies as a base for foreign investors to invest money in the country. There are three possibilities for such participation of foreign investors:

1. the establishment of a Hungarian company with foreign participation as shareholders;
2. the establishment of a wholly foreign-owned Hungarian corporation;
3. foreign investment in an existing Hungarian company.

A reasonable tax policy and a declaration of the state's responsibility to provide a guarantee of compensation to foreign investment are two other important factors to motivate foreign investments.

All aspects of this Hungarian program could be implemented in the Soviet Union. But this should be not only a Soviet move toward a more favorable regime for foreign investors. There is also the need to eliminate some barriers constructed in the past by foreign governments. There are some important restrictions on Soviet-U.S. trade. We will touch upon the four most important:

1. The Jackson-Vanik Amendment links most favored nation tariff status and other trade benefits to freedom of emigration. As a result of Jackson-Vanik, the Soviet Union has not received most favored nation status, has not participated in U.S. govern-

ment credit or credit guarantee programs, and has not signed a commercial agreement with the United States, with the exception of the grain agreement.

2. The U.S. government has not provided credit and other investment assistance for U.S. loans to the Soviet Union. There are two federal agencies providing such assistance, the Export-Import Bank (EX-IM) and the Overseas Private Investment Corporation (OPIC). EX-IM is the federal agency responsible for extending credits and guarantees at favorable rates to support exports. There have been some obstacles limiting EX-IM activity in the Soviet Union. For example, a 1986 amendment to the Export-Import Bank Act prohibits any EX-IM credit or guarantees in connection with a purchase or lease of any product by a socialist country. The Byrd Amendment sets a US\$40 million limit on any EX-IM loan or guarantee for the purchase, lease, or procurement of any product or service connected with research or exploration of fossil fuel resources in the Soviet Union.

OPIC is a government-owned corporation that provides political risk insurance for loans and supports U.S. investments abroad, mainly in developing countries. OPIC was also barred from doing business with the Soviet Union.

The Stevenson Amendment to the Trade Act of 1974 also limits EX-IM and OPIC involvement in investments in the Soviet Union. It prohibits any agency of the U.S. government other than the Commodity Credit Corporation, which issues guarantees to support exports of agricultural products, from approving any loans, guarantees, or insurance for exports to the Soviet Union in an aggregate amount in excess of US\$300 million without prior congressional approval.

3. There is no investment protection agreement between the Soviet Union and the United States that can provide mutual assurances that investment in the host country will not be expropriated or otherwise impaired or discriminated against by authorities of the host country, and that an adequate compensation will be paid in connection with any required taking, with recourse provided to arbitration before a neutral forum.

4. It is also important to adopt some improvements to the existing Soviet-U.S. tax treaty. For example, there is a serious problem

of exemption from host country taxation upon repatriation of investment profits, which reduces the possibilities for American partners in JVs to repatriate their profits because U.S. joint venture partners are subject to a 20 percent withholding tax under the Soviet law. Another problem is the assurance that fees or commission earned by U.S. companies for services to JVs where a U.S. company participates will not be taxed in the Soviet Union on the basis that the income was earned through the venture itself.

Stock and Commodity Exchange in the Soviet Union

Long-term borrowing through selling of bonds to pay for the construction of long-term projects should be started in the Soviet Union. Different kinds of securities, including shares, bonds, certificates of deposit, and commercial bills, should be issued by the central government, regional governments and authorities, and companies. These securities should be traded on central and regional stock exchanges in the Soviet Union and worldwide. We think that the best place for the central stock exchange (SE) in the Soviet Union is Leningrad. Regional exchanges can be opened in capital cities of Union Republics, including in Moscow, as the capital of the Russian Republic. From our point of view, given the conditions for the growth of nationalist movements in the republics, Leningrad would be a more neutral and acceptable candidate to house the central SE than would Moscow because Leningrad is an old symbol of the window to the West. Also, a regional SE should be opened in Vladivostok or Nakhodka on the Far East coast of the Soviet Union.

Each SE should be a limited liability or joint-stock company established by banks and other financial organizations on the basis of the law on shareholding companies. The organization and operation of each SE should be determined by the rules and regulations enacted by the SEs themselves. Each founder should contribute the stipulated amount of money to the SE's funds. Managing bodies should be established and authorized by the founding meeting of each SE: the SE Meeting, the SE Managing Board, the Supervisory Board, the Disciplinary Commission, and the Clearinghouse.

The SE Meeting should be a governing body that approves the annual financial report, determines the distribution of profits, and issues directives for future activity. The Meeting will elect members of other managing bodies of the SE and set up rules and regulations governing the SE's operations. The Managing Board will carry out the everyday work of the SE and prepare materials for SE Meeting sessions. The Supervisory Board will audit financial operations and annual financial reports. The Disciplinary Commission will supervise the work of the SE's bodies and employees and ensure regularity and orderliness in the SE's operations. The Clearinghouse will play a very important role in the SE's activities; securities owners will be able to deposit securities for safekeeping and collect interest and dividends on their bonds and shares.

Participants in SE operations may be legal entities and possibly natural persons who, according to specific criteria, will be accepted by the SE Managing Board. Those members will have the right to order stockbrokers to buy securities on their behalf and for their account, and on behalf and for the account of others.

Revenues of each SE will consist of brokerage fees and they can be used for investment, covering costs of operations, paying salaries to SE employees, and for other purposes on the basis of SE Meeting decisions. All SEs should operate under the control of a special government agency having the same set of rights and responsibilities as the Securities and Exchange Commission in the United States.

The process for creating commodity exchanges (CE) should also start from the creation of an appropriate set of rules and regulations that would be enacted by CEs concerning their organization and operations. For the control of CE operations, a special government agency with same functions as the U.S. Commodity Futures Trading Commission should be established.

Each CE would be a limited liability partnership or joint-stock company established by groups of banks and financial and industrial organizations operating in this sector of economy. The establishment and organization of each CE should be governed by the legislation pertaining to shareholding companies. Each CE should be a legal entity and be registered by the special organization.

Founders of CEs will invest some amount of money to serve as guarantees for exchange operations. The Clearinghouse of each CE should be organized on the basis of a strict examination of the creditworthiness of each candidate to membership in it.

The rules and regulations of a CE's operations should be prepared by founders and approved by the founding CE Meeting. This Meeting also will elect all managing bodies of the CE, probably similar to those of an SE.

While care must be taken in designing such organizations and selecting their members, it is critical to begin promptly the process of marketizing the Soviet economy.

13

Major Financial Obstacles to the Formation and Operation of Joint Ventures

Michail A. Portnoy

Financing the activities of joint ventures in the Soviet Union is one of the main problems that concerns western partners in the course of their economic cooperation with the Soviet Union. The main difference between joint ventures and Soviet enterprises is the joint venture's real independence, its ability to operate according to its own plans and business objectives. The principles of cost accounting, self-financing, and self-recoupment, which are set as goals to be reached by Soviet enterprises in the process of economic reform, are natural operating principles for the joint venture, and allowance for these principles is provided by Soviet joint venture legislation. Nevertheless, this situation is new and difficult for Soviet banks because they are used to performing control functions on behalf of the state rather than evaluating credits on the basis of commercial considerations.

Thus, Soviet banks found themselves in the new situation of having to deal with independent firms, and so they behaved very cautiously in order to protect their own interests as well as those of the whole country. As a result, Soviet banks continue to operate mainly as state rather than commercial banks. Another reason Soviet banks tread carefully when dealing with joint ventures is the absence of any experience with previous successful joint venture activities in the Soviet Union. From this point of view, joint ventures are also a new type of partner for Soviet banks. These two reasons—the independence of joint ventures and the absence of their previous successful activities—require Soviet banks to appraise the financing of projects submitted by joint ventures from the point of view of the project itself. Less attention is paid to the financial position and the reputation of the joint venture's founders, in spite of the fact that they can be the guarantors of the credits. Moreover, the project approach to investment financing is consistent with the bank's lending policies to Soviet firms.

The credit and account operations in rubles are carried out for joint ventures by Vneshekonombank (Bank for Foreign Economic Affairs) and by specialized banks. This process is far from convenient for joint ventures, as Vneshekonombank and the specialized banks are monopolies. The situation is not sustainable in the long run, and obviously it must be changed by developing the Soviet economic system. The commercial banks that are being founded in the Soviet Union must be given the right to deal with joint ventures in rubles as well as in foreign currencies. The most significant obstacles preventing Soviet commercial banks from providing credits to joint ventures in foreign currencies are their lack of funds and their lack of experience and skilled personnel.

Following the signing of the constituent documents of a joint venture and its registration with the Soviet Ministry of Finance, a joint venture as a legal entity is entitled to open accounts in banks and to request loans. Soviet banks provide credit to joint ventures involving partners from CMEA countries or from other countries on equal conditions. Special attention is given to the necessity of well-founded economic prospects to demonstrate the ability of the joint venture to repay the loans. Long- and medium term credits are most commonly issued for creating the production base of the joint venture.

Credits in rubles can be provided for joint ventures for industrial construction. The amount of the credit is limited by the projected total cost of construction, and the term of the loan is six years beginning from the first tranche. The rates of interest on long- and intermediate-term credits are established by Soviet banks at rates of 3 to 5 percent per year. Short-term ruble credits are given to a joint venture by specialized banks to meet current expenses. The credit limit is set by the banking institution in agreement with the joint venture. For the use of credit, the joint venture pays the bank interest at the rate set for the corresponding branch of the Soviet national economy. A procedure has been introduced for bank verification of security and repayment of credit, as well as for applying a number of sanctions in the event of violation of the credit terms.

A joint venture that has direct access to the foreign market may be given credits against export commodities from a separate loan account without limits on credit. Short-term credit, for a period of up to two years, is given in foreign currency to a joint venture to purchase abroad raw materials, auxiliary materials, and other commodities. The procedures for granting security and repayment of credit and payment of interest on the loan are analogous to those established for obtaining long- and intermediate-term credits in foreign currency.

At the beginning of 1990, joint ventures operating in the Soviet Union had received 68 credits. The volume of credits denominated in foreign currencies is currently US$1.2 billion. Vneshekonombank has provided 22 percent of this total, including the credits given by its affiliate in Zurich; the remainder was provided by foreign banks. In many cases, Vneshekonombank was not the sole creditor of joint venture projects but rather participated jointly with foreign banks. These foreign banks provided US$970 million for credits to joint ventures, 22 percent of which was guaranteed by Vneshekonombank. In such cases, Vneshekonombank provided counterguarantees from Soviet legal experts, who in practice assumed all the risks connected to the projects. Such guarantees were undertaken in extraordinary cases in order to accelerate the terms of fulfillment of specific projects.

The financing of joint ventures from foreign sources was carried out approximately in equal proportions at fixed and floating rates of interest. The average margin for credits was about 1 percent, its fluctuation depending on the reliability of the projects and the ease in securing credits. Credit terms also depended in large part on the projects, the duration of which ranged from a few months to more than ten years.

Most joint ventures were founded on the basis of funds contributed by the partners, a tendency that corresponds to the goals the Soviet Union seeks to achieve by attracting foreign partners for cooperation. This is also in accordance with the common approach for financing new projects—the expenditures and risks are met mainly by the founders, while creditors mostly are concerned with the repayment of credits. In some cases, however, the partners create joint ventures with the minimum required funds, expecting to finance their projects, sometimes very grandiose ones, with bank credits. Such joint ventures have a slight chance of achieving their objectives if the creditor banks or financial experts do not choose to take part in the project. It is important to take into account that joint ventures are responsible for their obligations with all their property, according to the Decision of the Council of Ministers No. 49 of January 13, 1987. In this regard, the Foundations of Civil Legislation of the Soviet Union are not applied to joint ventures.

As a rule, Soviet banks lend on the security the commodity-material values that are the objects of credit, but, if essential, the collateral may take the form of other property in accordance with Soviet legislation. This condition is recorded in the documents the joint venture presents to the bank in opening an account. Credits can be guaranteed by the guarantees of the joint venture's founders. If the founders are unable to provide such guarantees, they may be provided on the Soviet side by ministries, departments, and banks, and by foreign firms and banks on the side of the foreign participants. The granting of credits is based on a bank analysis of the economic state of the joint venture. Sometimes the bank's staff may participate in the foundation of the joint venture, thus providing their expertise at an earlier stage.

The partners of the joint venture must pay greater attention to the real value of the existing facilities in order to receive financial support from outside sources. There are numerous examples of significant efforts and expenditures made to elaborate projects that could not obtain outside financial support, especially in foreign currencies. These situations arise because it is relatively easy to obtain credits in rubles. Indeed, the Soviet credit system provides a huge surplus of ruble funds. At the beginning of 1989, Soviet enterprises had balances of free funds—the largest source of credit funds—of about 100 billion rubles. Many new commercial and innovation banks have easy access to such funds and can provide credits in rubles for joint ventures. The situation with foreign currency funds, however, is quite the opposite.

It is rather obvious to predict that the evolution of the Soviet credit system in the course of economic reform will lead to changing conditions for lending to joint ventures. Receiving credits in rubles will become more and more difficult, and the rates of interest will increase to 6 to 8 percent for short-term and 7 to 9 percent for long-term credits.

One of the most difficult problems is lending to joint ventures in foreign currencies. Credits in foreign currencies in the Soviet Union are issued by Vneshekonombank, the Moscow International Bank, the International Bank for Economic Cooperation (IBEC), and the International Investment Bank (IIB). The latter two act, in this case, as foreign banks.

The joint venture can also obtain foreign currency credits from foreign banks and firms. To obtain credits from foreign and international banks or to deposit its own funds in these banks, however, the joint venture must first receive a license from Vneshekonombank, a requirement established by the Decision of the Council of Ministers of March 7, 1989, "On the Measures for State Regulation of Foreign Economic Activities." The license is a written permission for a specific operation, with indication of its main conditions. Before granting the license, Vneshekonombank examines the viability of the operation and the presence of a sound economic basis for its fulfillment, but the bank takes no responsibility for the success of the operation. The primary reason for licensing the operation is the lack of experience of many Soviet participants in the economic arena. Is it understood that the requirement for licensing is provisional, but it is difficult to say when it will be eliminated. The decision on licenses for operations involving large sums of money is made by the Council of the Vneshekonombank. During 1989, about forty licenses were given by Vneshekonombank for different monetary operations, including for the operations of joint ventures.

Although the ruble is inconvertible, it is natural to carry out some measures of monetary control, and its forms must be clear for domestic and foreign partners. The existing volume of joint venture crediting in the Soviet Union does not meet their needs completely, because each kind of crediting has its own limits, which in turn are connected to the current state of the Soviet economy.

Joint ventures can generally obtain credits in rubles in adequate amounts and without obstacles. This does not mean, however, that the joint ventures can purchase for these rubles the commodities they need. The problem is not the absence of such commodities;

indeed, they may exist, but they are distributed by planning bodies and not traded in a free market. Thus, the underdeveloped market relations that characterize the Soviet economy thwart the success of joint ventures. Nevertheless, the situation is not entirely hopeless. We expect that the measures undertaken by President Gorbachev to accelerate economic reform will promote the resolution of this problem.

Obtaining and using foreign credits is more complex and difficult due to the state of the Soviet balance of payments. It is obvious that until the ruble is convertible, the Soviet government cannot permit the free transfer of funds in foreign currency for capital and credit operations. It is also clear that in such a case the Soviet Union would experience uncontrolled growth of its external debt. Moreover, as world practice indicates, the free movement of capital can be permitted only by the most economically developed and powerful countries in the world economy. The Soviet Union has to come a long way before it becomes such a country. During the next ten to twelve years, a significant goal would be to achieve ruble convertibility on the current account. Therefore, at least during this period, the control for obtaining foreign credits by joint ventures on Soviet territory will be maintained, a situation that must be realistically accepted.

Western partners consider the Soviet level of external debt a potential point of contention. While the problem is very real, the true difficulty lies not so much in the level of Soviet indebtedness, which is rather small, but in its structure. Official sources report that Soviet foreign debt was 34 billion rubles as of mid-1989. Although some Soviet financial experts contend that about half of this sum consists of regular short-term credits for financing the external trade, their opinions cannot be confirmed because of the lack of Soviet statistics. In any case, the financial side of the Soviet external debt is overestimated in both the West and in the Soviet Union. The political side of the problem improved after Mikhail Gorbachev became president and radical steps were taken to accelerate the economic reform. Thus, the creditworthiness of the Soviet Union remains strong, or at least acceptable.

There still exists the problem of Soviet export growth and its structure. In this field also, the main improvements can be expected from radical economic reforms and other steps promoting the activities of foreign capital, including joint ventures.

It is time for Soviets to abandon the practice of insisting on preferential interest rates on foreign credits. As is well known, the western partner compensates for such concessionary credit terms by increasing the prices of the delivered commodities.

Foreign partners also believe that the joint venture's method of currency accounting creates obstacles for the transfer of profits abroad. To earn enough currency for its expenditures in foreign currency, including bonus payments to foreign specialists, the joint venture has to export a portion of its products, which conflicts with the foreign partners' intent to operate mostly on the Soviet market. Indeed, it is clear that exporting the joint venture's product requires much effort to compete on the world market. Despite opposition from western quarters, Soviet authorities assume that by being obligated to export its products, the joint venture will maintain modern technology and equipment in its enterprises. The hardcurrency constraint is partly eliminated by the possibility of the joint venture buying commodities on the Soviet market in order to export them abroad, which means that the activities of the joint venture are partly rewarded in the Soviet Union in the form of barter.

Some problems also arise from currency exchange. If this order were to be established by the authorities only, it would generate problems especially for those joint ventures that carry out expenditures and receive profits partly in rubles and partly in foreign currencies. Soviet enterprises dealing on the world market have no such problems because they carry out their payments in the currency of the partner's country or in some international currency such as the dollar.

For the western partners of the Soviet joint venture, currency problems weigh heavily. For the western partner, the ratio of the profit received in hard currency to the capital invested in the joint venture is one of the most important indicators. The western partner is concerned primarily with the disproportions that arise from the difference between the level of the costs of production in the Soviet Union and world prices because of the incorrect rate of ruble exchange. A lesser concern for western participants is the risk associated with exchange-rate fluctuations for foreign currencies that always exist in the world markets. The foreign partner of the joint venture thus has to constantly compare its costs and profits in rubles with the same values calculated in hard currencies. The resolution of this problem is also related to the problem of ruble convertibility. Indeed, it is rather a difficult problem, but it can be solved within a reasonable period of time.

There exists as yet no common tax legislation for joint ventures. The rules of taxation are currently described in a number of different documents, though it is to be expected that further experience will yield the basis for correcting the existing rules before final tax legislation is elaborated. The present system of taxation for joint ventures is based on the following normative acts: the Decision of the Council of Ministers No. 49 of January 13, 1987; the Instructions of the Ministry of Finance No. 124 of May 4, 1987; the Decision of the Council of Ministers No. 1405 of December 2, 1988, and No. 203 of March 7, 1989. The tax rate for the joint venture is 30 percent of the net profit. The profit subject to taxation is calculated in the following way: The balance profit is used to make deductions to the reserve fund, as well as to other funds of the joint venture intended for developing production and science and technology by the normative rate set in the constituent instruments. Insurance premiums are also paid out of the balance profit. The sum remaining after these deductions is the profit on which tax is paid to the state budget. The tax is remitted to the state budget in rubles in four equal parts during the taxable period. A delay in payment of the tax is penalized by a charge of 0.05 percent for each day of delay.

A joint venture is provided with some privileges in terms of taxation. First, it is exempt from the tax on profit during the first two years from the time of declaring a profit. (Declared profit is profit indicated on the balance sheet of the enterprise). Those joint ventures operating in the Eastern Economic Zone of the Soviet Union are exempted from the tax on profit during the first three years. They also are granted a reduced tax rate on profit, set at 10 percent. The Ministry of Finance is given authority to apply reduced tax rates or completely exempt a joint venture from the tax on profit. Such privileges are granted to a joint venture if it has acquitted itself as a dependable exporter of products, is oriented toward manufacturing products in an area of priority to the Soviet economy, is manufacturing import-substituting products, and is introducing progressive technologies.

This system of taxation has some shortcomings, some of which are the result of outmoded Soviet accounting methods, which differ substantially from those in the West. In particular, the Soviet system of accounting is based on the cash principle rather than on the economic principle accepted in western countries. Therefore, the balance profit obtained on the basis of Soviet methods may differ substantially from the figure that would be obtained by accepted methods of western accounting. The difference in the profit figures can also arise from the different aims of accounting. The Soviet accounting system is geared toward providing information for a variety of state agencies, while the western system focuses on the needs of the firm. Soviet authorities are working on the question of clarifying the procedure for accounting the profits, but this task is rather difficult, and it will take some time for a mutually acceptable set of accounting procedures to evolve.

REPATRIATING THE WESTERN PARTNER'S PROFIT

The profit left after the previously mentioned settlements is divided between the joint venture partners in proportion to their capital shares. Foreign partners are guaranteed the transfer of profit in foreign currency owed them following this distribution. The question of the concrete forms of profit transfer involves certain difficulties. Because the accounting of the joint venture is kept in rubles, the profit of a foreign partner subject to transfer is expressed in rubles in the joint venture's accounts. Profit transfer in this case can be effected in the following ways:

1. A joint venture functions on the principle of complete self-recoupment in hard currency. Its balance account with the Bank for Foreign Economic Affairs contains sufficient sums to meet the demands of the joint venture in the process of its operation and to pay the foreign partner its share of profit in foreign currency. In this case, the share of profits in rubles owed to the foreign partner is converted to the appropriate currency at the exchange rate set by the State Bank on the day of the transfer

abroad. The resulting profit in foreign currency is remitted to the foreign partner from the balance account of the Bank for Foreign Economic Affairs. The repatriated profit is taxed at a rate of 20 percent, unless an alternative procedure has been negotiated in an interstate agreement. For example, for residents of Italy the tax rate is 15 percent, in accordance with the Soviet-Italian tax agreement. For joint ventures in the Eastern Economic Zone of the Soviet Union, the tax rate is 10 percent. Income reinvested in the same or other joint ventures or used for purchasing commodities in the Soviet Union in order to export them abroad is tax free.

2. In the event of inadequate hard-currency receipts from exporting products, a joint venture may rely on receipts from sales on the Soviet domestic market for foreign currency. Purchases for foreign currency are made out of the foreign currency resources of enterprises or the centralized foreign currency sources of the ministries.

A major problem with Soviet taxation rules is the difficulty accounting for some expenditures that are common for the western firms but virtually unknown to Soviet partners, for example, advertising, promotional activities, and losses of unrepaid credits that are to be written off. Also unclear are the tax liabilities incurred if the joint venture is liquidated.

The further success of joint ventures in the Soviet Union will depend, as do other progressive economic reforms, primarily on the success of perestroika, which must be assured during a reasonably short time.

Part III

Rewriting Soviet Business Law

14

Draft of Joint Venture Law (March 5, 1990)

Soviet Ministry of Justice

MODIFIED DRAFT

Law of the Soviet Union on Joint Ventures Created on the Territory of the Soviet Union with the Participation of Soviet and Foreign Legal Entities and Citizens.

I. GENERAL PROVISIONS

This law establishes special applications of Soviet law regarding the creation and activity on Soviet territory of enterprises with the participation of Soviet legal entities and foreign legal entities and citizens (hereinafter referred to as "joint ventures").

Article 1. Joint ventures are created for the purpose of more complete satisfaction of the country's demand for products (work, services), raw materials, and manufactured goods; the introduction into the Soviet economy of advanced foreign technology, management experience, and additional material and financial resources;

Thanks are due to Emily Silliman for providing Geonomics and its seminar participants with this draft revision of the Soviet joint venture law just as the seminar began. This draft provided the seminar working group members with the latest Soviet business law proposals and thus became the primary basis for the working groups' recommendations and the summer workshop's ultimate draft law.

The translation was prepared from a text dated March 5, 1990. Translation is courtesy of ASET Consultants, 8350 Greensboro Drive, Suite 805, Maclean, VA 22101.

the development of the country's export base; and production of imported goods.

Article 2. Joint ventures may perform any type of activity that fulfills the goals foreseen in the foundation documents, with the exception of activity that is against the laws of the Soviet Union and Soviet republics.

Certain types of activity of the joint venture can be undertaken only on the basis of permission (licenses) issued according to procedure established by Soviet law. The permission may stipulate the conditions for engaging in such types of activity.

Article 3. Joint ventures are legal entities according to Soviet law.

Joint ventures organize their activity on the basis of cost accounting, self-financing, and hard-currency self-sufficiency.

Article 4. Joint ventures may create on a voluntary basis sectoral, intersectoral, regional, and interregional associations of joint ventures.

Joint ventures may participate in concerns, consortia, intersectoral state associations, various associations and other large-scale organizational structures created on a voluntary basis by Soviet enterprises, associations, and organizations.

The provisions of this law apply to the activity of associations of joint ventures assigned the rights of legal entities and also to associations and other forms of organizations engaged in commercial activity voluntarily created by Soviet enterprises and organizations with the participation of joint ventures.

Article 5. Joint ventures are governed in their activity by the Soviet Law "On Stock Organizations, Other Economic Associations and Companies" and other legal acts of the Soviet Union and Soviet republics regulating the activity of Soviet state enterprises, with the exceptions stipulated in this law.

Specifics of the creation and activity of joint ventures involved in banking activities are set forth in the Soviet Law "On Banks and Banking Activities," the Soviet Law "On the Soviet Gosbank," and also other acts of union republics concerning banking activities.

Article 6. If after ratification of the present law laws are adopted that worsen the conditions for joint venture activities, the joint ventures established prior to the existence of such laws will be subject to the laws in effect at the moment of registration of the joint venture.

The provisions of this article do not apply to those Soviet legislative acts that set taxation.

Article 7. The present law applies to the establishment of international economic joint ventures with participation of Soviet and foreign organizations, companies, and administrative bodies on Soviet territory.

Article 8. If international agreements of the Soviet Union set new rules that differ from those of the Soviet Legislature, joint ventures will follow the rules of the international agreements.

II. REGISTRATION OF JOINT VENTURES

Article 9. Joint ventures are established on the basis of agreement between participating parties with permission of the local authorities of the joint venture location. The procedure for obtaining permission for such joint ventures is set by the Soviet republic. Such permission will be given to one of the Soviet participants in the joint venture.

Joint ventures are created as joint-stock companies, as companies with limited liability, and as other types of economic companies and organizations.

In cases stipulated by the law of the Soviet Union and Soviet republics, joint ventures are established with the permission of the indicated state organs.

Article 10. Participants of joint ventures with the Soviet Union can be legal entities:

1. state enterprises, associations and organizations;
2. public organizations, unions, and their enterprises and organizations;
3. manufacturing cooperatives, their unions, and their enterprises and organizations;
4. leasing enterprises;
5. concerns, consortia, interbranch state associations, associations, other organizations that are not part of the system of state or-

gans, and public organizations; and

6. other organizations in cases specified by laws of the Soviet
   Union and Soviet republics.

Joint ventures can establish a new joint venture with participation of a Soviet enterprise, organization, or association on condition of making a contribution of not less than US$100,000 into the charter fund. This rule is applied when a joint venture becomes a member of a Soviet association of enterprises, associations, unions and organizations, concerns, and consortia of intrabranch state associations.

Foreign participants of joint ventures can be state authorities, companies, and other enterprises that are legal entities in their country of origin, and also can be physical persons, having in accordance with the law of the country of which they are citizens, or in which they maintain permanent residence, the right to undertake such activity.

Article 11. The decisions on creation of joint ventures are made by state organs, state enterprises, associations, and organizations with the agreement of the superior organ.

Public organizations themselves make decisions on the creation of joint ventures, and enterprises of public organizations make decisions according to procedure established by the central organs of those organizations.

Production cooperatives make decisions on creation of joint ventures with the agreement of the Council of Ministers of the Soviet republic without regional *(oblast)* division of the Council of Ministers of the autonomous republics, the Kray Ispolkom, oblispolkom, Mosgorispolkom, and Lengorispolkom, depending on the location of the cooperative, or with the agreement of the ministry or department to whose enterprise the cooperative is attached.

Joint ventures and other organizations not included in the system of state organs or public organizations make decisions on creation of joint ventures on their own.

Article 12. It is established that the state organs and central organs of public organization during the decision of the question on creation of joint ventures consider the following obligatory requirements:

1. attainment of the joint venture of economic self-sufficiency, including hard currency, in accordance with the presented feasibility study; and
2. conformance of the feasibility study of the joint venture to environmental protection standards.

Article 13. A response to a proposal by the Soviet participant for creation of a joint venture will be given by the corresponding organ or central organ of the organization no less than thirty days from the moment of the receipt of the proposal in written form.

The agreement and charter of the joint venture must also contain the following:

1. purpose of activity;
2. participants (founders);
3. name, location of headquarters, and affiliates;
4. timeframe for establishment;
5. size of the charter fund, respective shares of the partners, size of contributions by participants, schedule for contributions to the fund, and procedure for distributing the joint venture's profits and losses;
6. the rights of the participants;
7. management and oversight organ's subjects of their conduct and procedures for their activity;
8. appointment of the organ to which the joint venture's accounts are sent and which will be required to facilitate access by the business community;
9. procedures for accounting; and
10. basic procedures for liquidation of the enterprise.

Article 14. Joint ventures are considered created and acquire the rights of a legal entity from the day of their registration.

Registration of joint ventures, one of whose participants is an enterprise of union significance, is effected by the Soviet Ministry of Finance.

Registration of the remainder of joint ventures is effected by financial organs according to procedure determined by the law of the union republics.

In the course of registration, the documents presented are: the agreement on creation of the joint venture and its charter; the technical feasibility study; verification that the foreign participants are legal entities; verification from the foreign participants' banks that the foreign partner is solvent (conscientiousness as a bank client); the receipt from a Soviet bank confirming the transfer by the participants of a sum of money required for formation of the charter fund (not less than 25 percent of the amount established in the charter); and other necessary documents depending on the type of activity of the created joint venture, including the production feasibility study, design documentation for construction, and so forth.

The registration of joint ventures and their affiliates requires a payment in the amount established by the law of the Soviet Union and the union republics.

The creation of joint ventures is announced in the press.

III. PROPERTY AND FUNDS OF THE JOINT VENTURE

Article 15. The ownership by foreign participants of a joint venture is not limited by percentage (the relative proportion will depend on the size of the joint venture, on the branch of the national economy, and on other factors) but by absolute size in the sum equivalent to US$100,000. In the case of creation of an affiliate, the minimum investment of the joint venture must be US$50,000.

Article 16. The joint venture has its own property, necessary for conduct of the activity as stipulated in the foundation documents.

The property rights of the joint venture are defended in accordance with Soviet law. Penalties on the property of the joint venture may be imposed only by the decision of organs that in accordance with Soviet law may examine disputes involving joint ventures.

The provisions of part two of this article are applied also to the property of the foreign partners of the joint venture, received by them as a result of joint venture profit distribution and also tied to the reduction by them of the share of the joint venture, or through withdrawal from the joint venture or its liquidation, and also assets imported into the Soviet Union as a partial contribution to the charter fund.

Article 17. The property of the joint venture can be used to answer for all of its obligations, including loans. In this capacity, rights contributed by the participants into the charter fund—including for use of land, water, and other natural resources, buildings, structures, equipment, and other property rights—can be used.

Special permission must be received from Soviet or republic organs to transfer rights to minerals or continental-shelf resources.

The property set forth may be sold by creditors according to agreed upon prices, including at auctions by Soviet organizations, and in cases covered by law of the Soviet Union and its republics and by foreign legal entities and citizens.

Article 18. The joint venture's property must be insured by Soviet insurance organizations. Risk insurance for joint ventures is obtained from insurance organizations according to the partners' agreement.

Article 19. The joint venture creates a reserve fund and funds needed for its operation and the development of its work force.

The reserve fund is created in an amount established in the foundation documents, but it cannot be less than 25 percent of the charter fund. The formation of the reserve fund is effected by means of an annual contribution in Soviet or foreign currency until the size of the fund established in the foundation documents is reached. The amount of the annual contribution to the reserve fund is covered in the foundation documents, but it cannot be less than 5 percent of the balance-sheet profit.

The list of other funds and the procedures for their formation and expenditure are determined by the joint ventures themselves.

Article 20. The formula for amortization deductions is stipulated in paragraph 33 of the Soviet Council of Ministers Decree of January 13, 1987: "Amortization deductions are conducted in accordance with current instructions for Soviet state organizations if another method is not stipulated in the foundation documents."

IV. DOMESTIC AND FOREIGN ECONOMIC ACTIVITY OF JOINT VENTURES

Article 21. The joint ventures develop and confirm programs for their economic activity themselves.

Joint ventures have the right to undertake state orders on a voluntary basis through concluding contracts with the corresponding state organ, including on a competitive basis.

The state organ in this case is responsible for supplying to the joint venture limited centrally allocated material-technical resources, construction, and contract work necessary for fulfillment of the contract and to guarantee to the joint venture a market for the products, work, and services covered in the state order. The joint venture is obliged to fulfill the contract for delivery of the products, completion of work, or services covered in the state order.

Article 22. Delivery to the joint venture of centrally allocated products of Soviet production is effected through the Soviet participant and its superior organ in full accordance with the demands of the joint venture. For other products, their delivery to the joint venture is effected on the basis of agreement with the producers, trade organizations, and material-technical supply, and also through the retail network of state and cooperative trade.

The type of currency in the accounts and the pricing is determined by the joint venture in agreement with the suppliers of the products.

The purchase of material resources essential to the joint venture is effected on the foreign market by the joint venture itself, through the foreign participants, or through Soviet foreign trade organizations using hard-currency resources of the joint venture.

The sale of products (work, services) of the joint venture is effected by the joint venture itself, not including cases covered by Article 21 of this law.

Article 23. Joint ventures can only export products (work, services) they produce themselves and import products (work, services) only for their own needs. They may also effect operations with raw material received in accordance with regulations established for Soviet enterprises.

Export and import operations of the joint venture are effected on its own, through foreign economic organizations, or through the marketing network of the foreign participants in the joint venture.

Article 24. All hard-currency expenditures of the joint venture, including payment of profit and other sums, accruing to the foreign participants and specialists must be made in hard currency from the joint venture's account.

Article 25. Property imported into the Soviet Union during the period covering the charter documents as a contribution to the charter fund is not subject to customs payments.

Article 26. The foreign participants in the joint venture are guaranteed transfer abroad of sums in hard currency that accrue to them as a result of the distribution of profits of the joint venture and also in connection with reduction of their share in the joint venture, either by withdrawal from or liquidation of the joint venture.

The profit of the foreign participant in rubles cannot be transferred and can be expended only on the territory of the Soviet Union through its ruble account or through reinvestment.

V. PROTECTION OF INVENTIONS AND INDUSTRIAL MODELS

Article 27. Exclusive rights to inventions and industrial models, created by workers of the joint venture in connection with the fulfillment of the work assignments, belong to the joint venture on the basis of a contract concluded with the worker at the time of hiring.

According to the agreement, the worker relinquishes to the joint venture rights to receive patents for inventions and industrial models created by the worker in connection with his work assignments, and the joint venture is obliged to pay the worker a reward.

Patents are issued in the name of the joint venture, with an indication in the patent of the last name, first name, and middle name of the inventor.

Joint ventures themselves make decisions on the patenting in foreign countries of their inventions and industrial models according to procedure established in the foundation documents.

VI. CREDIT AND ACCOUNTS

Article 28. Joint ventures may keep their money in any bank on Soviet territory, and they may keep foreign currency in those banks on Soviet territory empowered by law of the Soviet Union and its republics and in foreign banks with the permission of Vneshekonombank.

The procedure for conducting accounts, percentage deductions, and effect of payments is established in agreement with the bank that conducts the corresponding account.

The exchange-rate difference in hard currency of the joint venture and also for its operations in hard currency are transferred to the account of its profits and losses.

Article 29. Joint ventures may use credit on commercial terms set forth in rubles by any bank on Soviet territory, and in hard currency by any bank on Soviet territory thus empowered by the laws of the Soviet Union and its republics or foreign banks and firms.

Article 30. The writing off of monetary assets from the accounts of the joint ventures is conducted only through their instructions or by decision of organs that in accordance with Soviet law may examine disputes involving joint ventures.

Article 31. Banks granting credits (including foreign banks) have the right to verify the use of the credit issued to the joint venture as its collateral.

VII. TAX OBLIGATIONS OF THE JOINT VENTURE, TAX REDUCTIONS, VERIFICATION OF PENALTY TAXES

Article 32. Tax obligations of the joint venture and its participants, tax reductions, and verification of the correctness of tax penalties and penalties on arrears are regulated by legal acts of the Soviet Union on taxation issues.

VIII. JOINT VENTURE PERSONNEL

Article 33. The personnel of the joint ventures are primarily Soviet citizens. The administration of the joint venture is obliged to conclude agreements with the trade union associations created at the enterprise. The content of these agreements, including provisions for development of the work force, are determined by Soviet law and the foundation documents.

Article 34. The labor relations of persons working at the joint venture are regulated by laws of the Soviet Union and the union republics on labor in accordance with this law.

Joint ventures themselves determine procedures for hiring and firing workers, forms, systems and amounts of wage payments, schedules for the work day, shifts, calculating work time, and holiday and vacation time.

Joint ventures themselves determine the length of the yearly paid vacation, but its length cannot be less than that established for similar categories of workers at state enterprises.

Article 35. Social security (with the exception of the pension funds for foreign workers of the joint venture) and social insurance for workers at the joint venture are regulated by norms established by Soviet law.

The Soviet State Committee for Labor and Social Issues of the USSR has the right to determine special applications of Soviet law on social insurance for foreign workers of the joint venture.

The joint venture contributes to the Soviet state budget an amount for state social insurance of Soviet and foreign citizens and contributions to the pension funds of Soviet citizens according to norms established for Soviet organizations. Payments into pension funds for the foreign workers are made into the corresponding funds of the country of which they are permanent residents in the hard currency of that country.

Article 36. Wages for the foreign workers of the joint venture are taxed at the rate and according to procedures established in Soviet laws on taxation of the population.

The nonexpended portion of these wages in hard currency may be transferred abroad.

IX. OVERSIGHT OF JOINT VENTURE ACTIVITIES

Article 37. Financial and other state organs within the limits of their competence verify the adherence of the joint venture to laws, including payment of taxes and other contributions to the budget, conduct of accounting procedures, foreign economic activity, protection of labor, technical safety, environmental protection, and protection of historical monuments and culture.

Joint ventures annually present to local financial organizations the joint venture's annual accounting balance in the form of a balance sheet, account of profits and losses, addendum to the balance, and explanatory notes. The procedure for presentation of these documents is determined by the Soviet Ministry of Finance.

Article 38. Joint ventures can hire auditing organizations to verify their financial and commercial activity.

Article 39. Joint ventures are not obliged to present any sort of accounts or information to foreign state organs. If necessary, foreign participants inform their country's organs about the result of their participation in the activity of the joint venture.

X. LIQUIDATION OF JOINT VENTURES

Article 40. Joint ventures may be liquidated in cases of divergence of the joint venture from the goals outlined in the foundation documents; inability to maintain hard-currency self-sufficiency; inability to form the charter fund within the timeframe and in the amount permitting the beginning of operation of the joint venture within a year of the date of its registration by the Soviet Ministry of Finance; and other reasons covered by legislation of the Soviet Union and the union republics.

Article 41. The foreign participant in the case of withdrawal from the joint venture or its liquidation reserves the right to receive its contribution in the form of money or goods for the remaining cost at the moment of withdrawal or liquidation, after all obligations have been met to Soviet participants and third parties.

Article 42. Liquidation of joint ventures is regulated by the financial organs with which the joint venture was registered. For liquidation of the joint venture, a liquidation commission is appointed by the Soviet Ministry of Finance. Notice of liquidation is published in the press.

XI. DISPUTES

Article 43. Disputes between joint ventures and organizations with Soviet state, cooperative, and other public organizations, internal disputes, and disputes between participants of the joint venture on issues connected with its activity are taken to the Soviet courts, or by agreement of all sides, taken to a court of arbitration, or in cases stipulated in Soviet law, taken to organs of state arbitrage.

15

The Need for a
Foreign Investment Law

Keith A. Rosten

The Soviet-U.S. working group drafted a law on foreign investment as the next logical step in efforts to attract foreign investment to the Soviet Union and its constituent republics. The Soviet Union adopted joint venture legislation in January 1987, marking a watershed in the Soviet Union's foreign trade relations. This joint venture decree signaled a fundamental shift in how foreigners could conduct business in the Soviet Union. The Soviets expected that this joint venture legislation would attract massive amounts of foreign capital to revive their moribund economy.

Although there has been great western interest in the potential of the Soviet market and its 290 million consumers, expected capital investment has not materialized. The economic climate and the obstacles created by the Soviet bureaucracy, along with political instability and uncertainty, have slowed western investment. Soviet joint ventures account for less than 5 percent of Soviet foreign trade flows, and the potential for foreign investment remains largely untapped.

Recognizing the failure of joint venture laws, the Soviet Union is attempting to create a more accommodating legislative environment for foreign investors. In June 1990, the Supreme Soviet adopted a new enterprise law, one of several laws needed to promote a stable legal environment for both domestic and foreign investment. Two competing versions of a foreign investment law for the Soviet Union have been drafted recently as another step to encourage foreign investment.

191

The governments of the fifteen constituent republics of the Soviet
Union have also been keenly interested in providing a suitable environment to attract foreign investment. The Geonomics working
group chose to draft a progressive foreign investment law for one of
the republics, the Russian Republic. We thought that this far-
reaching, liberal legislation would receive prompter and
friendlier consideration in the more reform-minded Supreme
Soviet of the Russian Republic than in the Supreme Soviet of the
Soviet Union. Despite its focus on the Russian Republic, this draft
can serve as a model for other republics, outlining the cooperative
relations that the constituent republics may wish to develop. An
explanation of the major provisions of the draft law is set out below,
followed by the actual text of the draft law in chapter 16.[1]

APPROACH

The Geonomics working group set out to draft a law to:

1. attract foreign investment to the Russian Republic;
2. extend protection and guarantees to foreign investors;
3. establish a mechanism for repatriation of earnings; and
4. create a regulatory authority that minimizes barriers to foreign
   investors and makes the approval of foreign investments quick
   and simple.

DEFINITIONS

To achieve these objectives, we define foreign investment expan-
sively: essentially, anything of value transferred to a business entity
or unit in the Russian Republic by a foreign investor qualifies as
foreign investment.

The draft law treats similarly all entities with more than a
minimal amount of foreign investment, but it creates a few exceptions in registration procedures, areas of permissible operation,

---

1. A Russian translation of the draft law is available through the Geonomics
Institute. Both versions are authoritative, though they are not direct translations.

and susceptibility to state orders. For these particular purposes, the draft law distinguishes among three kinds of entities based on varying levels of foreign participation.

"Domestic Companies" with foreign investment are those companies with more than a minimal foreign share. For these companies, the share of foreign participation is from 5 percent to 20 percent of the Russian firm's capital.

"Mixed Companies" occupy a middle tier where the percentage of foreign investment is 20 percent or more but not more than 70 percent.

A "Foreign-Controlled Company" is one in which the share of the foreign investor is more than 70 percent. The draft law specifically allows 100 percent foreign ownership. The draft law refers to these three types of entities as "Foreign Investment Companies."

The draft law does not treat as Foreign Investment Companies those entities with less than 5 percent foreign participation. Branches of foreign legal entities are generally entitled to treatment similar to that of Foreign-Controlled Companies.

PROTECTION AND GUARANTEES

The draft law sends a clear signal that all Foreign Investment Companies are entitled to no less favorable treatment than that of firms with no foreign participation. The draft also provides the foreign investor with common protections against expropriation and nationalization, even absent governing treaties between the Russian Republic and foreign countries. Under international law, if a state expropriates or nationalizes foreign investment, the foreign investor must receive prompt, effective, and adequate compensation. The draft law captures this principle in its provisions.

MINIMAL STANDARDS

Foreign Investment Companies and Foreign Branches should not be relieved of their responsibilities and duties under domestic law. They must obey all relevant laws, including those in the sensitive areas of environmental protection and social security, and they shall not offer working conditions to their labor force that are inferior to those currently established under applicable Soviet law.

DIFFERENTIAL TREATMENT

In certain areas, Foreign Investment Companies and Foreign Branches are entitled to treatment more advantageous than that available to domestic firms. Republic authorities may extend incentives to foreign investors so long as these do not adversely affect other Foreign Investment Companies or Foreign Branches.

Labor

The Foreign Investment Company and Foreign Branches should not be inhibited from providing additional incentives to their work force. The draft law specifies four areas in which Foreign Investment Companies and Foreign Branches should not be constrained by current law. These are:

1. limits on wages and other compensation;
2. compensation and other benefits in hard currency;
3. employment and discharge; and
4. intellectual property rights.

The draft law grants flexibility to Foreign Investment Companies and Foreign Branches not only in compensating employees but also in hiring and firing employees. These provisions enable employers to provide strong incentives to their labor force yet also assure them a measure of flexibility in their operations. The provision on intellectual property allows employers and employees to negotiate whether patent and trade secrets should be assigned to the employers, which is not currently allowed under Soviet law.

Central Planning Tasks

An essential element of current joint venture legislation is that joint ventures are not subject to orders from the central planning system. This principle is incorporated into the draft law so that central planning authorities cannot dictate tasks to Mixed and Foreign-Controlled Companies and Foreign Branches, though these entities may voluntarily accept orders from the central planning authorities. Because the foreign participation in Domestic Companies is not substantial, by definition less than 20 percent, this principle does not apply to these companies.

Customs Duties

The draft law exempts Foreign Investment Companies and Foreign Branches from paying customs duties on capital contributions in the form of equipment, machinery, or materials. This was done so that cash and other contributions, including equipment, machinery, and materials, would be on an equal footing. This policy should encourage Foreign Investment Companies to import equipment, materials, and machinery, contributing to the industrial base of the Republic. To prevent Foreign Investment Companies from acting as brokers, the exemption does not apply if the machinery, equipment, or materials are imported for resale.

Repatriation of Profits

The cornerstone of the draft law is a mechanism by which the foreign investor can easily repatriate profits. Under current law, absent an applicable treaty, the foreign investor must pay a tax of 20 percent on repatriated earnings. The draft law eliminates this tax and provides an easier mechanism not only to repatriate hard-currency earnings but also to convert ruble earnings into hard currency.

The draft law sets no limitation on transferring abroad profits, dividends, royalties, or capital. The only limitation is on the ability of the Foreign Investment Company or Foreign Branch to generate hard-currency earnings, including rubles converted into hard currency through currency exchanges with other Foreign Investment Companies, because only accumulated hard-currency receipts can be transferred.

The draft law also provides substantial incentives for those Foreign Investment Companies and Foreign Branches generating rubles. Foreign investors may convert ruble dividends into foreign currency at the official rate. Moreover, foreign investors may sell or exchange ruble profits to other foreign investors for hard currency at mutually agreed on rates.

RESTRICTIONS

The draft law reflects the fact that there are certain areas that most countries view as having national security considerations or other significant public interests. Foreign investments in these areas require a higher level of concern. Accordingly, the draft law bars Foreign-Controlled Companies and Foreign Branches from participating in certain areas of the domestic economy, such as national defense, television, and insurance, and it requires Council of Ministers' approval for other Foreign Investment Companies to engage in activities in these areas.

REGISTRATION

The draft law establishes an Office of Registry of Foreign Investment ("Office of Registry"), which is charged with maintaining a Registry of Foreign Investments (the "Registry"). The draft law adopts a declaratory system of registration. The Office of Registry may only reject an application for procedural reasons—failure to complete the form properly, for example—but cannot exercise any other discretion over the registration of foreign investment. If the Office of Registry fails to act within thirty days, then the application is considered approved.

We considered two possible alternatives. One alternative was to require Foreign Investment Companies to register under the domestic corporations or partnership laws first, and then, to take advantage of the benefits of the Foreign Investment Law, to register separately under this law. The other alternative, which is the view that we ultimately adopted, was to require registration only with the Office of Registry. We wanted to eliminate the necessity to register under other domestic registration requirements. Accordingly, once registered in the Registry, the entity acquires a legal status, without the necessity of registering elsewhere.

BANKING AND ACCOUNTING

One major hurdle that joint ventures have faced is the Soviet banking system. The draft law makes it clear that foreign investors may maintain both ruble accounts and hard-currency accounts.

Currently, joint ventures are required to combine rubles and hard currency in financial statements for the Ministry of Finance. The hard currency is translated at the artificially deflated official rate of exchange. Hence, the financial statement does not reflect the financial condition of the joint venture.

Although Foreign Investment Companies and Foreign Branches will continue to maintain a separate set of books for ruble transactions and hard-currency transactions, the taxing authority must charge a tax based on some measure of earnings. We decided to translate hard currency into rubles at the official exchange rate, recognizing that this would promote exporting enterprises. Foreign Investment Companies and Foreign Branches should still have a substantial incentive to earn rubles because of the mechanism for transferring rubles into hard currency provided by the draft law.

RELATIONSHIP TO INTERNATIONAL LAW

This law has a number of international implications, including the Russian Republic's relations with the other constituent republics. The law presupposes a fundamental principle of international law that is already embodied in the Russian Republic Civil Law that all treaties prevail over any contradictory provisions of this law. If there are no applicable treaties, the draft law will fill the gaps.

The draft law cannot magically solve all the problems facing the Russian Republic or the Soviet Union, but it does frame the fundamental issue of how to open the Russian economy to the world

198 THE EMERGING RUSSIAN BEAR

market. Only after careful and serious debate in the Supreme Soviet of the Russian Republic can the draft law's vision become reality.

16

Draft Foreign Investment Law: Russian Soviet Federative Socialist Republic

Geonomics Institute

I. GENERAL PROVISIONS

Article 1. Definitions of Foreign Investment

Investment means the transfer of value by a foreign investor to an existing or newly created business entity or units on the territory of the Russian Soviet Federative Socialist Republic (RSFSR).

Investment may take the form of shares of stock and other forms of equity interests and may be acquired either directly from the issuing entity, which may be an existing entity or a newly formed entity, or from third persons in exchange for value, including money (in the form of Soviet rubles or foreign currency), land, buildings, equipment, materials, technology, patents, licenses of inventions, know-how, management, and other tangible and intangible property. Establishing a branch by a Foreign Investor is an investment under this law.

"Foreign Investors" include stock companies, partnerships, and other legal entities and citizens, entities without citizenship, and also Soviet citizens living abroad and having income from foreign organizations and citizens.

Legal entities organized on the territory of the RSFSR and having more than 50 percent direct or indirect foreign ownership shall be deemed to be Foreign Investors for the purposes of this law.

The investment of legal entities formed and registered in other republics of the Union of Sovereign States taking place in the RSFSR, and also the investment of citizens of other republics, is not considered foreign on the condition that the laws of the corresponding republic do not consider as foreign the investment made by legal entities and citizens of the RSFSR.

A "Domestic Company" means any stock company or partnership established and registered in the RSFSR in which the share of the Foreign Investor in the equity capital is not less than 5 percent and not more than 20 percent.

A "Mixed Company" means any stock company or partnership registered in the RSFSR in which the share of the foreign investor in the equity capital is more than 20 percent and not more than 70 percent.

A "Foreign-Controlled Company" means any stock company or partnership in which the share of the equity capital Foreign Investor is more than 70 percent up to and including 100 percent.

Bonds, debentures, and other forms of indebtedness issued by stock companies that are at the will of the investor freely convertible into shares of stock are considered as equity interests. Such indebtedness shall be considered part of the stock company's or partnership's equity capital.

A "Foreign Investment Company" means Domestic Companies, Mixed Companies, and Foreign-Controlled Companies, and each of them.

A "Foreign Branch" means an internal subdivision of a foreign stock company or partnership organized and established under the laws of a foreign state that intentionally engages in business activity on the territory of the RSFSR.

Article 2. Scope of Coverage of Foreign Investment

Foreign-Controlled Companies may not engage in business activity in the defense branches of industry, in the branches of industry engaged in the extraction of precious and rare materials and minerals, and in the areas of insurance, television, radio, communications, and air and rail transportation in the national economy of the RSFSR.

Domestic and Mixed Companies may engage in business activity in the areas specified in paragraph 1 only with the permission of the Council of Ministers of the RSFSR.

Foreign investment in the branches of the national economy connected with the exploration and extraction of mineral resources requires permission of the Council of Ministers of the RSFSR and the consent of the Council or Councils of People's Deputies of the territory or territories on which the given activity will be carried out.

Foreign investment in banking may be carried out in accordance with the regulations established by the State Bank of the RSFSR and the Ministry of Finance of the RSFSR.

Article 3. Legislation on Foreign Investment

The legal regulation of foreign investment on the territory of the RSFSR is under the competent authorities of the RSFSR.

The basic provisions on foreign investment in the RSFSR are established under this law.

The relations connected with foreign investment and not covered by the present law are governed by the legislative acts of the RSFSR, and in their absence, the legislative acts of the autonomous republics.

The activity of stock companies and partnerships using foreign investment and of branches of foreign firms in free-trade zones on the territory of the RSFSR is governed by the laws of the RSFSR on these zones.

Article 4. The Legal Status on Foreign Investment

Foreign investment on the territory of the RSFSR enjoys legal protection. National treatment of the activity of legal entities governed by legislation of the RSFSR and the autonomous republics, with the exception of those provisions that concern exclusively Soviet organizations, is extended to Foreign Investment Companies and Foreign Branches. These exceptions shall grant a legal status to Foreign Investment Companies, including questions of owner-

ship of land used for business purposes, no less favorable than that
granted to legal entities having no foreign ownership.

The decision on attracting foreign capital into the capi-
tal/property of a stock company to be established or into an existing
stock company or partnership is taken in conformity with the
founders or the general meeting of the stockholders/partners.
Establishing Mixed Companies, Foreign-Controlled Companies,
and Foreign Branches is governed by Section II of this law.

Mixed and foreign companies have the right to accept on a voluntary basis state orders through making contracts with the corresponding organs.

Foreign Investment Companies may establish on the territory of
the RSFSR, in other republics of the Union of Sovereign States, and
in foreign countries companies, open branches, and representative
offices in accordance with legislation existing in these areas.

Foreign Investment Companies and Foreign Branches founded
in the RSFSR are governed by the laws of the RSFSR and autonomous republics and the regulations and decisions of the local
Councils of People's Deputies, including questions relating to the
protection of nature and social security for Soviet and foreign employees.

Profits and other income received by Foreign Investors can be
kept in accounts in rubles and foreign currency in banks of the
RSFSR and other republics of the Union of Sovereign States with
the right of use, and also in foreign-currency accounts in foreign
countries.

Article 5. The Rights of the Foreign Investor

In addition to the rights provided for by legislation for participants
of stock companies and partnerships, the Foreign Investor has the
right to transfer abroad dividends, income, royalties, and other
profits derived from foreign investment and also investment and
reinvestment of capital and of profits, money received from the sale
of stock, and transfer of contributions in partnerships.

Transfer of profits into foreign currency is carried out at the expense of accumulated hard-currency receipts of the corresponding

Foreign Investment Companies or Foreign Branches.

Given treaties of the RSFSR with other states on the protection of foreign investment, transfer by Foreign Investors of these sums abroad is carried out in freely convertible currency in accordance with concluded treaties.

The accounts of Foreign Investment Companies shall be denominated in rubles. The translation of current transactions and values in other currencies shall be made at the official exchange rate on the day or on the closest previous business day to the end of the company's accounting period or, if there is no applicable official rate, at the market rate.

The valuation of Foreign Investors' hard currency or hard-currency price contributions to or investments in Foreign Investment Companies will be valued in rubles at the then-applicable official rate or, if there is no applicable official rate, at the market rate in effect when such contributions or investments are paid in or transferred to the Foreign Investment Company.

Foreign Investors may convert ruble dividends into foreign currency at the official rate in effect at the time. Foreign Investors may also sell their ruble profits to other Foreign Investors for hard currency at freely agreed-to rates. Acquisition of hard currency by this means shall be accepted as hard-currency receipts for the purposes of Article 5, paragraph 2.

Foreign Investors receiving dividends and other income from Domestic Companies are completely relieved from paying taxes on the transfer abroad of this income in freely convertible currency.

Article 6. Privileges

Machinery, equipment, and other property imported to the RSFSR by or on behalf of a Foreign Investor in the form of investment is not subject to customs duties, provided, however, that such machinery, equipment, and other property is not for resale in the ordinary course of business.

Considering the significance for the national economy of the RSFSR of the separate forms of production (labor, services) produced by the enterprises of Foreign Investment Companies, Foreign

Branches, their labor capacity and large expenses for production, the Council of Ministers of the RSFSR has the right to establish privileges for individual Foreign Investment Companies or Foreign Branches in addition to privileges provided for in tax legislation, provided, however, that such privileges do not adversely affect the ability of other Foreign Investment Companies or Foreign Branches to carry out their business activities.

Article 7. Labor Law, Social Insurance, and Social Guarantees for Workers

Soviet legislation and legislation of the RSFSR on labor and relating to social guarantees for workers apply to Foreign Investment Companies and Foreign Branches with the exception of the following:

1. limits on wages and other compensation;
2. employment and discharge;
3. intellectual property rights; and
4. wages and other compensation in hard currency.

The administration of Foreign Investment Companies and Foreign Branches shall conclude agreements with trade unions in which there must be agreement on the questions enumerated above in paragraph 1. The agreement cannot worsen labor conditions, work, and rest of workers in comparison with analogous conditions established by legislation of the RSFSR.

The questions of social guarantees of Soviet citizens and of social insurance of Soviet and foreign workers is regulated by Soviet legislation.

Article 8. Government Registration and Registry of Foreign Investment

The Council of Ministers of the RSFSR shall establish an Office of Registry of Foreign Investments (the "Office of Registry"), which shall maintain a Registry of Foreign Investment (the "Registry").

Registration in the Registry is carried out by application to the Office of Registry.

Stock companies and partnerships legally constituted under the laws of the RSFSR acquire the status of Foreign Investment Companies from the moment of their registration and inclusion in the Registry, as evidenced by a certificate of registration.

If a new company, partnership, or other business entity results from the investment activity of a Foreign Investor, then registration will simultaneously create this new legal entity in conformity with existing laws of the RSFSR governing the creation and operation of such entities and grant it the status of Foreign Investment Company.

A Branch of a foreign firm has the right to carry out business activity on the territory of the RSFSR from the moment of its inclusion in the Registry, as evidenced by a certificate of registration.

Registration of foreign investment is carried out in accordance with the regulations established by the Council of Ministers of the RSFSR.

On receipt of the certificate of registration, the Foreign Investment Company or Foreign Branch shall not be required to obtain any other approval of any government agency to commence or carry out its activities, other than as may be required by laws and regulations applicable to all entities engaged in comparable business activities within the RSFSR.

The registration application shall contain the following:

1. the name and principal place of business of the registering company or partnership;
2. the name and principal place of business of each Foreign Investor or Investors and each person or large entity directly or indirectly having a controlling interest in the Foreign Investor; for the purposes of this draft law, controlling interest means the right to vote 50 percent or more of the outstanding shares;
3. the Foreign Investor's share of equity; and
4. in the case of indebtedness, the amount of debt.

The registration shall take place not later than thirty days from
the date of presentation of the application for registration supple-
mented by the documents required by law. In the absence of a decision on the registration in the prescribed form, the stock company, partnership, or branch shall be considered registered.

Registration can be denied on the basis of violation of the established procedure for the formation of a company or for noncompli-
ance of the foundation documents with required legislation.

The rejection of the registration for substantive reasons is not allowed.

Rejection during the established period shall be subject to judicial review.

The information contained in the registration application shall
be public.

The stated information in the Registry is recognized as authen-
tic unless there is a contrary decision of a court or arbitration that
comes into legal force.

Foreign Investment Companies and Foreign Branches shall
file a quarterly report with the Office of Registry in a form prescribed by the Office of Registry. All information other than that
specified above in paragraph 8 of this Article shall not be public.

Article 9. Control of Activity of Foreign Investment Companies
And Foreign Branches

State agencies in the areas of their competence shall establish reporting and auditing procedures for monitoring the compliance of
Foreign Investment Companies and Foreign Branches with legislation, including payment of taxes and other payments in the budget; carrying out accounting and statistical reports, including statistics on foreign operation; protection of labor, safety conditions, natural resources, the environment, historical monuments, and culture; and other areas of the activity of companies, partnerships, and
branches of foreign firms.

Each Foreign Investment Company and Foreign Branch shall
have its books audited annually in accordance with applicable generally accepted accounting standards.

II. PROCEDURES FOR ESTABLISHING MIXED COMPANIES, FOREIGN-CONTROLLED COMPANIES, AND FOREIGN BRANCHES

Article 10. Establishing Mixed Companies

Mixed companies, with the exception of those cases provided for in Article 2 of the present law, are formed without special permission by their registration in the Registry.

Article 11. Foreign Branches

A Foreign Branch that transacts business on behalf of its firm is not considered a legal entity according to the legislation of the RSFSR. It operates in the framework of the established activity of the foreign firm. Assets on its balance sheet are a constituent part of the assets of the firm. On its obligations, the branch of a foreign firm is liable with all of the assets belonging to the foreign firm. A Foreign Branch does not have the right to issue stock or bonds on the territory of the RSFSR.

A Foreign Branch operates on the basis of statutes approved by the foreign firm. These statutes shall not contravene legislation on the principles of business activity on the territory of the RSFSR.

The management of the Foreign Branch of a foreign firm is carried out by a general director appointed by the foreign firm.

Foreign firms' branches whose exclusivity activity are sites for taking orders for purchasing or selling goods on behalf of the firm are exempt from paying taxes on income and profits they receive.

Article 12. Procedure for Establishing Foreign-Controlled Companies and Foreign Branches

Foreign-Controlled Companies and Foreign Branches are established/opened with the permission of the Inter-Departmental Committee (Governmental Commission) on Foreign Investment in the RSFSR.

To receive permission for the establishment of a Foreign-Controlled Company and the opening of a Foreign Branch, one is required to submit an application and necessary documents prescribed by legislation on stock companies and partnerships (and for branches of foreign firms, the applicable provisions of the present law), in which there must be contained information enumerated in Article 8 of the present law, and also, if necessary, the consent of local Councils of People's Deputies on the operations of stock companies, partnerships, and branches of foreign firms proposing to carry out activities in the jurisdiction of the Council.

To the application on opening a branch of a foreign firm must also be attached the following documents: notarized or certified copies of the documents on the registration of the foreign firm in the corresponding country, including its articles of incorporation; the permission of the appropriate governmental organs, on the territory of which the firm is registered, if such permission is required for the opening of a branch in the RSFSR; and the resolution on opening the RSFSR branch passed by the foreign firm.

On the submission of the application set forth in paragraph 1, the Foreign Investors shall pay such a registration fee to the government of the RSFSR in freely convertible currency in an amount as may be established by the Council of Ministers of the RSFSR.

The application for establishing a Foreign-Controlled Company and for opening a Foreign Branch must be reviewed by the Inter-Departmental Committee (Government Commission) on Foreign Investment in the RSFSR not later than sixty days from the date on which it was received. The decision of the Committee (Commission) is final and is not subject to appeal.

The receipt of permission to establish a Foreign-Controlled Company or open a Foreign Branch does not relieve Foreign Investors from registration of the stock company, partnership, and branch of foreign firms as a legal entity in the procedure provided for in Article 8 of the present law.

III. Guarantees and Protection of Foreign Investment

Article 13. Guarantees

Foreign investment in the RSFSR is not subject to nationalization, expropriation, or confiscation, except in those instances that are connected with protecting the interests of society, are nondiscriminatory in application, and where due legal procedures have been observed in accordance with existing legislation.

On the nationalization or expropriation of foreign investment, in accordance with paragraph 1, the Foreign Investor shall be compensated by the state for the property taken. The property taken shall be valued at its current value, which shall be based on market prices, and in their absence, on the basis of financial information contained in the accounting documents of corresponding stock companies, partnerships, and branches of foreign firms.

Compensation shall be in rubles that are convertible in accordance with the provisions of Article 5.

Compensation for property taken from Foreign Investors must be made promptly but in no event later than three months from the date on which the decision was taken to nationalize or expropriate. Any amounts unpaid after three months shall bear interest at the market rate of interest existing in the Foreign Investor's country on the last day that payment was due.

Article 14. Protection of Foreign Investment

Commercial disputes between Foreign Investment Companies and other business entities operating on the territory of the RSFSR will be adjudicated by the courts and arbitral tribunals of the RSFSR as provided for by the laws of the RSFSR.

Disputes among Foreign and Russian Investors in a Foreign Investment Company will be adjudicated by courts of the RSFSR and arbitral tribunals, unless the statutes of the company or other agreement between the parties provides for arbitration in a third country.

Disputes between Foreign Investors and the government of the RSFSR arising from the interpretation and implementation of the provisions of law may for the protection of Foreign Investors be adjudicated according to a foreign investment treaty between the RSFSR and the domicile of the Foreign Investor. In the absence of such a treaty, these disputes shall be adjudicated by Soviet courts and arbitral tribunals or, at the option of both parties, through arbitration by an arbitral tribunal in a third country.

Index

Accounting,
  allocation certificates as units of, 65
  money as a unit of, 64-65
  shortcomings of Soviet, 173
  systems of, in Eastern Europe, 31
  uniform standards of, 79
Accreditation, need for improvement in, 53
Afghanistan, and the U.S.-Soviet Income Tax Treaty (1973), 60
Agroprombank (agriculture bank), 15
Albalkin, Leonid, 63
Allocation certificates, 65
Amendment,
  Byrd, Export-Import Bank Act (1974), 55, 160
  Jackson-Vanik, Trade Act (1974), 51, 52, 95, 105, 106, 159-60
  Stevenson, Trade Act (1974), 55, 160
Antidumping, laws on, 56
Arbitration, international, 59
Arbitration Court, Soviet Chamber of Commerce and Industry, 140

Baltic Republics, privatization in, 29
Bank accounts,
  foreign exchange, 53
  ruble, for foreigners, 53
Bankers,
  lack of experienced, in the Soviet

Union, 166
  value of credit risk ratings to, 84
Bank for Foreign Economic Activity.
  See Vneshekonombank
Bank for Foreign Economic Affairs.
  See Vneshekonombank
Banking,
  Soviet,
    changes in, 165
    encouragement of deposits and, 69
    and foreign financing, 18-19
    infrastructure for, 19
    and joint ventures, 103, 165-70
    recommendations for development of, 15-19
    reform of, 48, 71
  universal,
    as a model, 22-23
    in the Soviet Union, 75-76, 77-78
Bankruptcy, 14, 68
Banks, in the Soviet Union,
  branch, 15
  clearing, recommendations for, 35
  commercial, 48
  cooperative, 15
  government, 15
  independent central, need for, 15, 16-17, 48, 69, 72
  innovative, 15
  role of, and investment, 22
  savings, 64

About the Contributors

MICHAIL ALEKSEEV is a leading expert with the Soviet Ministry of Finance.

JOHN A. BOHN, JR., is President of Moody's Investors Service, New York, NY.

ALEXANDER L. KATKOV is Professor of Economics, Leningrad Institute of Finance and Economics.

DAVID H. LEVEY is Associate Director for Sovereign Risk, Moody's Investors Service, New York, NY.

PETER B. MAGGS is Professor of Law, University of Illinois School of Law, Champaign, Ill.

VIKTOR P. MOZOLIN is Senior Fellow, Institute of State and Law, Moscow.

VLADIMIR T. MUSATOV is Head of the Economics Department, Institute for the Study of the USA and Canada, Moscow.

WILLIAM ORR is Economic Correspondent for the *ABA Banking Journal,* a monthly publication of the American Bankers' Association.

PETER J. PETTIBONE is Partner, Lord, Day & Lord, Barrett Smith, New York, NY.

MICHAIL A. PORTNOY is Senior Research Fellow, Institute for the Study of the USA and Canada, Moscow.

KEITH A. ROSTEN is Managing Director, Accord Consulting Group, Mountain View, Calif.

FRANCIS A. SCOTLAND is Managing Editor, *International Bank Credit Analyst,* Montreal, Canada.

About the Editors

JOSEF C. BRADA is Professor of Economics at Arizona State University. After having received both a B.S. in chemical engineering and an M.A. in economics from Tufts University, Dr. Brada went on to receive a Ph.D. in economics from the University of Minnesota. He is currently the editor of the *Journal of Comparative Economics*, and he is a member of the Board of Trustees for the National Council for Soviet and East European Research.

MICHAEL P. CLAUDON is President and Managing Director of the Geonomics Institute and Professor of Economics at Middlebury College. He received his B.A. from the University of California at Berkeley and his Ph.D. in economics from The Johns Hopkins University. He is the author of numerous articles and books on economics, and he serves as series editor for the Geonomics Institute for International Economic Advancement monograph series.

List of Seminar Participants

David O. A. Aiello
President
Executive Customs Brokers
Toronto, Canada

Michail Alekseev
Leading Expert
Ministry of Finance
Moscow

Sergei Alexashenco
Leading Specialist
State Commission on Economic
   Reform
Soviet Council of Ministers
Moscow

Jose L. Ante
President
Bicol Agro-Industrial Export-
   Import Corp.
Philippines

Raymond Benson
Geonomics Trustee,
Director
American Collegiate
   Consortium
Middlebury, VT

John A. Bohn, Jr.
President
Moody's Investors Service
New York, NY

Vladimir Anatolievich Bokrovsky
Deputy Chairman
State Commission on Economic
   Reform
Soviet Council of Ministers
Moscow

Josef C. Brada
Professor of Economics
Arizona State University
Tempe, AZ

Charles Brophy
Senior Counselor
Hill and Knowlton, Inc.
New York, NY

Michael P. Claudon
President
Managing Director
Geonomics Institute,
Professor of Economics
Middlebury College
Middlebury, VT

James L. Cochrane
Senior Vice President and Chief
  Economist
New York Stock Exchange, Inc.
New York, NY

Steven Cunningham
Professor of Economics
University of Connecticut
Storrs, CT

Daris G. Delins
Chief Economist
County NatWest Australia Ltd.
Sydney, Australia

Daniel Dunson
Partner
Sullivan & Cromwell
New York, NY

Nikita Lvovich Dvoretz
Adviser
Division on Social and
  Economic Issues
Communist Party of the Soviet
  Union
Moscow

John S. Freidin
Vice President
Geonomics Institute
Middlebury, VT

Donald W. Green
Executive Vice President
Mercator Corporation
New York, NY

Peter Holmes à Court
Director
Heytesbury Inc.
New York, NY

Robert A. Jones
Chairman of the Board
Geonomics Institute,
Chairman Emeritus
MMS International, Inc.
Incline Village, NV

Alexander L. Katkov
Professor of Economics
Leningrad Institute of Finance
  and Economics

Henry Kaufman
President
Henry Kaufman & Company
New York, NY

Robert L. Krattli
President
Scott-European Corporation
Montpelier, VT

Geoffrey Lamb
Adviser, Strategic Planning
World Bank
Washington, DC

Ms. Marju Lauristin
Head, Social Democratic Party
Deputy Speaker of the Estonian
  Supreme Soviet

David H. Levey
Associate Director
  for Sovereign Risk Unit
Moody's Investors Service
New York, NY

Peter Maggs
Professor of Law
University of Illinois
  School of Law
Champaign, IL

James G. McGann
Senior Vice President
Executive Council on Foreign
   Diplomats
Bedford, NY

Viktor P. Mozolin
Senior Fellow
Institute of State and Law
Moscow

Vladimir T. Musatov
Head of Economics Department
Institute for the Study of the
   USA and Canada (ISKAN)
Moscow

William Orr
Economic Correspondent
ABA Banking Journal
Waterbury Center, VT

Anu Pärt
Managing Director
Estonian-American Chamber of
   Commerce
Estonia

Peter J. Pettibone
Partner
Lord Day & Lord, Barrett
   Smith
New York, NY

Michail A. Portnoy
Senior Research Fellow
Institute for the Study of the
   USA and Canada (ISKAN)
Moscow

Jenik Radon
Partner
Radon & Ishizumi
New York, NY

Robert Ramsson
Senior Analyst
United States Government
Falls Church, VA

Keith A. Rosten
Managing Director
Accord Consulting Group
Mountain View, CA

Vincent J. Ryan
Chairman
Schooner Capital Corporation
Boston, MA

Leonard Santow
Geonomics Trustee,
Managing Director
Griggs & Santow, Inc.
New York, NY

Rolf D. Schmidt
Chairman
Sharpoint
Reading, PA

Francis A. Scotland
Managing Editor
*International Bank Credit
   Analyst*
Montreal, Canada

James Shapiro
Director, Economic Research
New York Stock Exchange,
   Inc.
New York, NY

Sergei Sergejevich Shtarev
Division on Social and
   Economic Issues
Communist Party of the Soviet
   Union
Moscow

Gail Stevenson
Assistant Professor of
  Economics
American University
Washington, DC

Eric Stubbs
Harriman School of
  Management and Policy
SUNY Stony Brook
Stony Brook, NY

Graham Taylor
General Partner
Pillsbury, Madison & Sutro
San Francisco, CA

W. Paul Tippett
Former Chairman and Chief
  Executive Officer
American Motors Corporation
Ann Arbor, MI

Eugene V. Uljanov
Executive Vice President
Vneshekonombank
New York, NY

Vitaliy Verzhbitskiy
Economic Officer
Embassy of the Soviet Union
Washington, DC

Peter Vihalem
Chairman
Tartu University School of
  Journalism
Estonia